# DINNER WITH
## *Eleanor*

### HELEN NIEMTZOW PRATT

Post Hill
PRESS

Post Hill Press
New York • Nashville
posthillpress.com

Published in the United States of America
1  2  3  4  5  6  7  8  9  10

*I dedicate this book to my husband, Eli Pritzker,*
*and my children, Suzanne Pratt Davis, Elizabeth Pratt,*
*Nina Pritzker Cohen, Michael Pritzker,*
*my little dog, the late Prince Paris,*
*Perla Cevita, a refugee dog from the hurricanes*
*of Puerto Rico, who has been a great comfort to us,*
*and Thomas, my tabby cat.*

# Contents

*Introduction* . . . . . . . . . . . . . . . . . . . . . . . . . . . . . ix
*Preface*. . . . . . . . . . . . . . . . . . . . . . . . . . . . . . . . . . xi

## Part One: Channah Spector  1

Chapter 1: Channah's Stained Glass . . . . . . . . . . . . . . . .  5
Chapter 2: The Ghet . . . . . . . . . . . . . . . . . . . . . . . . .  8
Chapter 3: Barren. . . . . . . . . . . . . . . . . . . . . . . . . . . 13
Chapter 4: Leaving for Bremen. . . . . . . . . . . . . . . . . . . 16
Chapter 5: Arriving in Bremen . . . . . . . . . . . . . . . . . . . 19
Chapter 6: The Silver Spoons . . . . . . . . . . . . . . . . . . . . 21
Chapter 7: Finding Work . . . . . . . . . . . . . . . . . . . . . . . 24
Chapter 8: The Fox and the Grapes . . . . . . . . . . . . . . . . 26
Chapter 9: Installing the Window . . . . . . . . . . . . . . . . . 30
Chapter 10: Ticket to America . . . . . . . . . . . . . . . . . . . 34
Chapter 11: The Voyage to Philadelphia. . . . . . . . . . . . . 36
Chapter 12: Unpacking. . . . . . . . . . . . . . . . . . . . . . . . 38
Chapter 13: Sophie's House . . . . . . . . . . . . . . . . . . . . . 40
Chapter 14: Harris Pomerantz . . . . . . . . . . . . . . . . . . . 43
Chapter 15: The Courting of Channah . . . . . . . . . . . . . . 47
Chapter 16: The Proposal . . . . . . . . . . . . . . . . . . . . . . 51
Chapter 17: Stained Glass in Philadelphia . . . . . . . . . . . 54
Chapter 18: Carriage Rides with Harris. . . . . . . . . . . . . . 56
Chapter 19: The Wedding . . . . . . . . . . . . . . . . . . . . . . 61
Chapter 20: Moving into Harris's House . . . . . . . . . . . . . 64
Chapter 21: Channah's New Family . . . . . . . . . . . . . . . . 66
Chapter 22: Betrayal . . . . . . . . . . . . . . . . . . . . . . . . . 69

Chapter 23: Leaving . . . . . . . . . . . . . . . . . . . . . . . . . . . . 72
Chapter 24: Independent . . . . . . . . . . . . . . . . . . . . . . . . . 74
Chapter 25: The Baby. . . . . . . . . . . . . . . . . . . . . . . . . . . . 76
Chapter 26: Raising the Redheaded Child . . . . . . . . . . . . . 79
Chapter 27: Beatrice . . . . . . . . . . . . . . . . . . . . . . . . . . . . 82

*Part Two: Helen* 87

Chapter 28: 1960, First Day of Architecture School. . . . . . . . 88
Chapter 29: Meeting Mickey . . . . . . . . . . . . . . . . . . . . . . . 95
Chapter 30: Learning About the Pratt Empire . . . . . . . . . . . 98
Chapter 31: The Relatives of Roger Sherman Pratt . . . . . . . . 100
Chapter 32: The Meeting of Eleanor Roosevelt,
            Joseph Lash, and Trude Wenzel Lash. . . . . . . . 104
Chapter 33: The Venona Decryption. . . . . . . . . . . . . . . . . 109
Chapter 34: My Future In-Laws . . . . . . . . . . . . . . . . . . . 113
Chapter 35: Arrival for Dinner . . . . . . . . . . . . . . . . . . . . 115
Chapter 36: Eleanor's Apartment. . . . . . . . . . . . . . . . . . . 119
Chapter 37: Talking with Eleanor . . . . . . . . . . . . . . . . . . 121
Chapter 38: The Interview. . . . . . . . . . . . . . . . . . . . . . . 126
Chapter 39: Dinner with Eleanor . . . . . . . . . . . . . . . . . . 130
Chapter 40: Leaving Eleanor's . . . . . . . . . . . . . . . . . . . . 136
Chapter 41: The Wedding . . . . . . . . . . . . . . . . . . . . . . . 139
Chapter 42: Honeymoon . . . . . . . . . . . . . . . . . . . . . . . 142
Chapter 43: Returning to Philadelphia . . . . . . . . . . . . . . 150
Chapter 44: The Eleuthera Vacation. . . . . . . . . . . . . . . . 155
Chapter 45: The Legacy . . . . . . . . . . . . . . . . . . . . . . . . 157
Epilogue . . . . . . . . . . . . . . . . . . . . . . . . . . . . . . . . . 159

# Introduction

I married Roger Sherman Pratt in 1962, and with this marriage came a long list of new relatives and friends who were suddenly a part of my life. The persons relevant to my story are: Eliot Pratt, Roger's father; Gertrude "Trude" Wenzel Pratt Lash, Roger's mother; esteemed biographer Joseph P. Lash, Roger's stepfather; and Eleanor Roosevelt, former first lady and wife of U.S. President Franklin Delano Roosevelt.

With this marriage, I found myself immersed in a world of old money and high-stakes players. Later, to my surprise, with the release of the Venona decrypts that revealed a quest for Soviet-American agents, I stumbled upon an aspect of my history that has not been told before, at least, not told in this way.

And now, on January 26, 2018, as President Donald J. Trump visits Davos, Switzerland for the World Economic Forum, Mr. Trump speaks of globalization and the facetiously proposed tax cuts "for the rich to help the poor." I can't help but to think that the same human rights issues that were the cornerstones of Eleanor Roosevelt's Universal Declaration of Human Rights in 1948 with the United Nations are still relevant now.

The culminating event of these histories, the intertwining of Joseph Lash, the Pratt family, and the Roosevelts, resulted in my dinner with Eleanor just before my wedding to Roger Sherman Pratt. This dinner has stayed with me ever since and has ached to be recorded. It is so fascinating and important to me that although many years have passed since the marriage, the subsequent divorce, and another marriage, I cannot seem to forget about this family, especially Joseph Lash, Trude Wenzel Pratt Lash, and most of all, Eleanor Roosevelt.

How did these persons, their affairs, and their alleged espionage fit into my own family history twenty years before my marriage in 1962? I hope to capture the events and not lose them with the passage of time, nearly fifty-six years later.

The very first words Eleanor said to me that night at our private dinner were, "Tell me about yourself." So, let me do just that.

# Preface

I have plans. I am eight years old and living with my family in Freehold, New Jersey. My family included: Abraham Niemtzow, a skilled and compassionate dentist; my mother, Beatrice, a beautiful freckled redhead; and Richard, my younger brother who would become a physician to President George Walker Bush (and other notable people) and the inventor of Battlefield Acupuncture.

My destination is the Methodist church on West Main Street in Freehold for my Brownies' meeting. This explains the borrowed Brownie uniform, which I wore to school, minus the brown beanie. The uniform was lent to me by a friend, Virginia, and I am proud to wear it. Membership in the Brownies will lead me to be a Girl Scout. I hope to someday have my own uniform decorated with many badges.

My parents know that I am going to Brownies after school, but only I know my route from Hudson Street Grammar School to the Brownies' meeting at the Methodist church a few blocks away.

Clutching the dollar bill my parents gave me, I head to my first stop on Center Street. Should I buy the Clark Bar or go to the comic book store? I decide to buy both at the newspaper shop that faces Main Street. After a right turn at the corner of Main and Center Streets, I am right in front of the shop.

I love Archie Comics and the adventures of the characters Archie, Veronica, Betty, and Jughead. I buy the latest edition. I identify with Veronica, who has dark hair, bangs, and large brown eyes like me, and I imagine I will be just like her in a few years. I exit the store holding my new possessions close and make my way to the courthouse steps where I hope to sit, eat, and read during a pit stop before the meeting.

I know that behind the courthouse is the county jail. Mr. Kent, my next-door neighbor and a county detective, once took me there to see the jail. He even pointed out an accused murderer—a man with a little mustache who was sitting alone in a cell reading a book. I have always had a special fascination with murder stories, though this accused murderer was the only one I ever came close to. I hoped that he was innocent and just awaiting trial and exoneration.

Because of traffic, I cross Main Street earlier than I had planned. As a result, I have to keep walking to get a seat on the courthouse steps. There, I will peacefully sit, eat my candy bar, and read my new comic book before the Brownies' meeting started.

Suddenly, I hear, "Dirty Jew!" shouted directly at me. This disgusting pronouncement comes from a young girl, about my age, who is walking arm in arm with her mother. I am alone. The mother says nothing, not even "Shut up!"

All I can do is feel shattered. My purchases lose their importance. However, I do not cry. I go straight on to Brownies, forgetting about my Clark Bar and Archie comic book.

The words "Dirty Jew" will ring in my ears forever.

*Channah Spector,*
*Helen's grandmother,*
*at age thirty.*

## PART ONE

# Channah Spector

Everything I know about my grandmother Channah Spector was told to me by either my mother or by grandmother herself. I was only seven years old when she came to live with us in Freehold. What I remember most is how much she loved us: Mom, Dad, Richard, and me. I always wanted to be put to bed by her because at this time she told me bedtime stories in Yiddish.

Yiddish is a language spoken by Jews in central and eastern Europe, mostly before the Holocaust. A mixture of German and Hebrew, it was, in essence, a universal language for the Jewish people. If you spoke Yiddish, you could travel all over the world, as

*Map of Georgia.*

my grandmother did, communicating in Yiddish. She went from Tbilisi, Georgia to Bremen, Germany, and then to America. Most of her communication was in Yiddish.

My grandmother's home country of Georgia was inhabited for thousands of years, since before the rise of Mesopotamia, an early civilization. It was a land no larger than the state of West Virginia and rich in culture and religious diversity. It was bordered by the Black Sea to the west, a meeting point for Africa and Europe. Along with the sea, there are the Surami Ridge and Likhi Range mountains to the north of the capital city, Tbilisi. It was the setting for many Greek mythologies such as the play *Prometheus Bound*, presumably written by Aeschylus.

When the Romans conquered the territory of Georgia, they referred to it as "farming,"[1] in their native language of Latin due to its rich soil. This was the origin of the name that Georgia comes from. Its people are very religious, with many relics of Christianity and Judaism. During the fourth Century A.D., Christianity became popular in Georgia and even took a lead during the Crusades, which occurred from 1096 to 1291 A.D.

There was also a Jewish and Islamic presence in Georgia, but it was minimal. There was a divide between Georgian and Ashkenazi Jews in the country. Georgian Jews lived separately from everyone and had different practices and languages. The Ashkenazi Jews lived in Tbilisi and were of Eastern European descent. These three religious groups, Christians, Jews, and Muslims, lived in Georgia, which was a little over twelve hundred miles from Jerusalem, an important city for each religion.

Many Georgians took a pilgrimage to Jerusalem to visit holy sites. Unfortunately, there was great religious intolerance that took place in the country. The pogroms,[2] for example, were violent acts of anti-Semitism. Many Jews escaped from Georgia due to this violence. In the early twentieth century, many Georgians came to America, where they could practice their religion freely and find new economic opportunities.

However, Channah left Georgia for a different reason. She left the man she loved, her husband Jacob, because she could not get pregnant. She was barren. This horrified her. She was an outcast in her society because of her condition.

At my young age, I wondered what it was to be barren. It was the thing that drove her from her family, her city, and her home

---

[1] "Farmer" in Latin is *agricola*. "Farming" in Latin is *agriculturae operum dabant*.
[2] Pogroms are organized massacres of an ethnic people, particularly of the Jews in Russia and Eastern Europe.

country of Georgia. What was barren? What caused this abnormal situation? Was it a malady?

I did not know the cause of her problem. It must have been a great force that made her move from all she ever knew. She had to leave because the terrible humiliation of her barrenness. She had to find refuge in America. Many people were leaving their homeland of Georgia in the early twentieth century for political reasons. Some went to America. Some went to Palestine, which later became Israel. It must have been a strong force to justify such a move at a time when traveling was so difficult.

My grandmother, with great determination, knew what she had to do. She had to go to America. What else could she do? She was a woman with only the training of glass staining, which she learned from her father, my great-grandfather, Revan Zev Spector.

Speaking only Yiddish, maybe some Georgian as well, she was on the move. She had to leave. There was no home for her in Georgia. Leaving was her only option.

# 1

## *Channah's Stained Glass*

When she was a young girl, Grandma Channah walked barefooted to the tsar's cousin's mansion to meet her father when his day's work was over. Revan worked hard as a stained glass designer not just because he needed a dowry for Channah, but because he also had to support all of his family. He liked his work. Channah was so beautiful, tall with flowing auburn hair and skin as pale as milk. The tsar's cousin told Revan, "You won't need a dowry for Channah. She is very beautiful." Channah heard this as she accompanied her father home from work with a basket of wild berries for her mother.

Channah felt exhilarated by the work she did with her father. His stained glass windows were absolutely beautiful. She liked participating in the design of the stained glass as well as the manufacturing and installation process. She learned how to arrange the glass segments to tell a story. Despite the fact that she was a woman, Channah considered herself the heir to her father's business.

*The City of Tbilisi, Georgia.*

Each day, Channah took a different route to and from work. She always brought a treat, such as a bundle of flowers or a basket of berries, home to her mother. She was careful to take only things that were in season. When grapes were ripe, her father pressed them into delicious fresh grape juice to be turned into wine. Wine wasn't the only thing that her father would make, though. He would dry the fruits and store them for the winter as well.

The tsar's cousin, Prince Gruzinsky, lived in the mansion where Channah's father worked. Revan depended on this work to make a living and support his family. The prince oversaw the design of Revan's stained glass windows, and he encouraged the themes of the windows to tell a story to the observer.

He wanted Revan to include creation epics from the Bible and other religious sources in the windows. This was difficult for Revan to depict. He was familiar with the Bible but only the epic

*Gruzinsky family coat of arms.*

of Adam and Eve. He had heard of the Babylonian creation epic, Enúma Eliš,[3] a water-based story that was not similar to any other stories. The tale didn't offer any symbolism for Revan to depict in a stained glass window, which made his work much harder.

---

[3] This ancient Babylonian epic is based on the creation of two water gods, Tiamat of salt water and Ea of fresh water, who gave birth to the seven continents.

# 2

## The Ghet

Tbilisi, the capital city of Georgia on the Kura River, was known for its stained glass production. Many of the themes for the stained glass designs were from Aesop's Fables. I remember my grandmother telling me the fable about the fox and the grapes. The story was about a fox that tried to eat a bunch of grapes hanging from a vine that did not belong to him. Try all he might, the grapes remained out of his reach. Eventually the fox gave up, with the excuse that the grapes were probably sour anyway.

My grandmother told me the story of the fox in Yiddish. I loved all of her stories and ran down the stairs at our home in Freehold to tell my parents about the fox in this story. But, it did not go over well with Mom and Dad. I wondered why. It turned out that when I pronounced "fox" in Yiddish, it sounded very much like an offensive curse word.

My memories of my grandmother and her stories are very thin and I haven't expressed them in a very long time. Yet I still

*Example of residential stained glass in Tbilisi, Georgia.*

feel an overwhelming love for my *bubbe*.[4] I am amazed at her strength, both physical and emotional. I still try to emulate her in many ways.

Channah had moved back to her parents' house, a little cottage with a fireplace and dirt floors whose only required maintenance was a light sweeping by a feather broom. The floors of the cottage were made of pounded earth from years of being trampled by boots. The cottage was divided into business and residential sections to accommodate her father's work[5] and his family's living quarters.

Channah had to leave Georgia and the man she loved because she was disgraced. *Bubbe* was anguished. She could not have a

---

[4] Yiddish for "Grandmother."
[5] The process of making a stained glass window starts with sketching a design. With the sketch beneath the glass, Revan would cut the glass and then sand down the edges. Once the edges of each piece were sanded, copper was placed along the edges so the pieces could be soldered together and framed.

child. She could not get pregnant and it was assumed to be her fault. To avoid the wrath of her mother-in-law, who felt deprived of a grandchild, my grandmother had to leave Georgia.

Some beautiful stained glass art was found in certain residences of Tbilisi. They had bright, strong colors and were geometric in design. It was made by Revan Zev, Channah's father. This glass was very valuable and was found only in churches and in some residences like her father's employer's castle on the Black Sea. Revan Zev lived in his small house with his wife and children, three girls, Channah, Sophie, and Rachel.

All Revan's work was done to support his family. Included in his struggles are the three daughters born to Nessa, his wife. His family of girls would make his life easier in his later years.

Don't think that Channah didn't feel the guilt from a wasted dowry. What happened to all the pride that Channah had? She was so beautiful she wouldn't need a dowry. Now Channah needed a dowry in a way she never expected. The dowry now belonged to her ex-husband and no return of it took place at the *ghet*. There was nothing fair about a *ghet* for the woman. All property accumulated in the marriage went to the husband.

The rabbi decided who was awarded certain items. Channah ended up with two large silver spoons, four silver forks, some pillowcases, two watches, and a broken bracelet.

Could it be that a "*ghet*" was actually a "got" when division of the property was decided? No longer was everything divided in half. The man must remain financially intact to start another family. The woman was cast off and no longer marketable.

Channah had no one waiting for her. She had depleted her family's reserves. Her dowry was wasted and another one was not to be forthcoming. This was another reason to leave Georgia.

Shocking as it was, Channah found it best to leave and that's exactly what she did.

There was no shortage of tears. Channah's sisters were devastated. Were they next? Barren? A stigma ever incurable and always a woman's fault.

Channah contracted smallpox just after she and Jacob divorced. If a person was lucky enough to survive it, they could be left scarred. Her weakness and the bed where she was confined kept even the doctor away. The vaccination for smallpox had not reached Georgia yet. The spread of smallpox brought fear and worry about being infected. So sick, Channah knew that she could die from the disease.

Channah's parents were beside themselves with worry seeing her bad luck continue even though she was so good to everyone. First, it was this childless marriage of such a beautiful young woman who couldn't stop helping others. Then, from nowhere, the devastating illness appeared. Beautiful Channah lay in her girlhood bed, banished from her marital bed. Given a *ghet* by their rabbi and no word from Jacob. How could he behave like this when he professed such love for Channah?

How could Jacob stay away from Channah, even though his family told him that he should forget her? A few days after the illness started there was a knock on the front door of Channah's parents' cottage. The door, usually unlocked, had been tightly shut. The neighbors were worried that their children would catch the disease from Channah and insisted that she be kept in isolation.

Carrying a lantern, Jacob threw open the front door and made his way into the dark cottage. He shined the light in front of Channah's face, which was surrounded by her beautifully embroidered pillows. Jacob said, "Channah, Channah, it's Jacob. The lantern is in front of your face." She only opened her eyes slightly and saw his face. Jacob said, "You are fine! Your face is not scarred by the pox." He said nothing more. Jacob was relieved to see that Channah looked okay.

The man she loved for so long could do no more. She couldn't cry. He left her parents' house and the life they had together for ten years was officially over. Channah thought of this moment frequently, but she didn't cry anymore.

She knew she had to leave and face life for herself.

Channah recovered from the smallpox and decided to leave Georgia and all of its overwhelming religious rules. She felt the pain of rejection and could only use her own power to find a new life in a new world. It was a journey out of the hell of nineteenth-century Georgian beliefs. She could not get far enough away from the foolish disgrace that came from ignorance and weakness.

# 3

## *Barren*

Channah left Tbilisi's port to begin her journey to Bremen, Germany after much discussion about the best way to go to America.[6] She decided Bremen would be a midway point to rest and further evaluate her journey at length. In the meantime, she tried to be in communication with her younger sister, Sophie, who had already made the trip to America and was living in Philadelphia. Sophie did not feel forced to leave Georgia the way Channah had, but was driven by the need for adventure. If Sophie would have stayed at home with her parents and younger sister, she would have eventually suffered the pogroms and after that, the Holocaust.

Channah was desperate to leave. She could not walk down the street, let alone go for tea, without being confronted with questions or suggestions about her failed marriage.

---

[6] In 1910, when Channah arrived in America, there were 13,515,900 immigrants in the nation. Information provided by the Migration Policy Institute.

Why couldn't she have a baby? Maybe she was just too tall to be fertilized. Was her husband so agitated over his mother's demands and her need for a grandchild that he couldn't approach Channah sexually? Channah's mother defended her and suggested almost daily a means to attract the young couple to each other that was acceptable by the mikvah.

The mikvah was a religious bath taken seven days after a married woman's menstrual cycle ended. It was necessary in order to be considered "pure" again for sex. Later, I realized that Channah's problems had to do with her issues with infertility. I suspected that Channah ovulated before the Mikvah bath, resulting in her inability to have children. Although Channah obeyed all these religious rules, she still could not get pregnant. The mikvah was thought to be prescribed by God.

Jewish women accepted and obeyed the ritual. Having a baby was a holy experience; in fact, the whole process of bringing a child into the world is considered special. Every step of the process had to be performed just so. It was short of having the rabbi present in the room while the couple had sex. No sneaking around was allowed; all this is to preserve the husband's assumption that the child is his. The ritual allowed for no illegitimate children and protected the paternal responsibility.

Intercourse was performed almost entirely for procreation. If one enjoyed it, this was an accidental byproduct and almost sinful. Somehow, Channah and her husband were not connected. It was decided that Channah was at fault. Isn't it always the woman who was blamed in childless marriages?

The raging ignorance in Channah's community drove her away. Her husband agreed to keep her home. He believed his mother's insistence that Channah was too uncontrollable to get pregnant.

Channah took little advice from anyone and obeyed all the rules. Unfortunately, they were contrary to her ability to get pregnant.

Channah planned to stop in Bremen on her way to America. It was better to leave all her troubles behind and catch up to Sophie in Philadelphia, the City of Brotherly Love. It was there that she would have more independence than in Tbilisi.

Revan told Channah, "I have a friend in Bremen named Rabbi Sheer. I will write to him and tell him you are coming. He has a large house and is happy to take in travelers for any length of time."

# 4

## Leaving for Bremen

Rabbi Sheer answered immediately, and Channah packed the little that she owned into a carpetbag and wrapped some loose change in a handkerchief. She carried about 249 *lari*[7] on her person, and the few items she was able to get from her husband she put in her bundle. She didn't have much and left in a hurry.

The *ghet* set Channah free, free to leave Georgia, free to go far away from Jacob so she would never speak his name or hear it spoken.

Channah made her decision to leave with automatic determination; leaving in disgrace was not an option. Disgrace gave her motivation. It was the only good thing about disgrace. Channah pounced on this determination.

Making an effective departure remained essential in her mind. Her goodbyes were brief. Deciding what to take with her

---

[7] $100 in today's currency. As of 2018, one Georgian lari is equal to $0.40 USD.

was limited to what she could carry. What was hers to bring? The *ghet* had reduced her possessions to the silver she brought into the marriage, her embroidery, her clothing, and fragments of her trousseau clothing no longer of use. The pretty nightgowns were no longer necessary for a surprise encounter. With love and the anticipation of becoming a bride, pillowcases were made by hand and were once a treasure. These items were now outdated and pointless. She would not need them in her new life. There was nothing else to do but remove herself from the unjust blame.

Channah got to Bremen by train and boat, and maybe even horseback to get from her village to Tbilisi. She did a lot of walking over familiar ground. Her steps were heavy. She did not want to leave disgraced and with the terrible burden of being barren. She had to leave everything behind her and she thought distance from her problems would serve to replenish her strength.

The only thing an anxious woman could do was sail by small boat from Tbilisi to Bremen and from there go to the United States. At the Tbilisi port of Batumi, Channah boarded a boat to Bremen.

Charting passage to Bremen was expensive, time-consuming, and hard for a woman who spent her entire life in a small town, nestled among loving parents and a talented artisan father. There was also the need for acquiring money for the journey.

My grandmother had left for Bremen with a well-thought-out plan. She took the carefully embroidered pillowcases and a beautiful valise. She wore one dress and wisely packed another. An emphasis was put on material objects that were wearable, safely keeping vulnerable valuables in her pockets or sleeves, such as her silver tablespoons. Coats with big sleeves and pockets were good for transporting Russian Nikolai gold. Channah's flatware would provide her with money at a future time. The transportation of silver was akin to the movement of gold throughout Eastern and Middle Eastern Europe.

Channah's height served to protect her. When she was finally on the ship, the layers of clothing she wore to avoid carrying a suitcase gave her the appearance of power. Even aggressive men thought twice about taking advantage of her. Her few belongings were still in her possession, except for her cash, which had been spent.

There were scoundrels everywhere and even Channah's carpetbag attracted the worst of them. Channah was wary about making new friends. When Channah slept on boats and trains, she shielded herself with a blanket. She kept all of her more important possessions with her under the blanket. It was getting dirty, but she couldn't do without it long enough to wash and dry it. "Why didn't I bring two?" she asked herself.

After Channah got to Bremen, she communicated home by postcard and letter. This gave her satisfaction because Channah was never able to express her emotions. It gave her back the strength that had been stolen from her by her failed marriage.

# 5

## Arriving in Bremen

*Kaus da mir, Rebe Sheer wohnt? De shule vie ist uo?*
Can you tell me where the synagogue is?

There was much questioning in Yiddish. *Vo ist de shule?* My grandmother could not speak or read English. Yiddish was all that she knew. The communication barrier produced a ghastly struggle, but she was not alone.

Everywhere in America, schools were created to make it possible to learn English for when people came to America.

Rabbi Sheer was a sacred man who helped travelers in Bremen. His house was located close to the docks where Channah's small boat from Georgia landed. On her journey from Tbilisi to Bremen, Channah had to change to several different fishing boats until she finally reached Bremen.

Bremen was not a place that Channah knew anything about. How will she find a way to America? The answer was always Bremen. "Why Bremen?" she asked. She learned that she had to have a place to wait for her paperwork to be put in order before journeying across the Atlantic. When she arrived on the docks in Bremen, she asked, "Is there a *rebbetzin*?" Not wanting to deal with the rabbi alone, she wondered whether the rabbi had a wife, a *rebbetzin*. It would be more proper if the rabbi was married. Channah, exhausted from the difficult journey from Tbilisi to Bremen, discovered that her money was depleting. She struggled to bring her few possessions with her to the rabbi's doorstep.

Fortunately, the rabbi found that many people traveling to America needed a safe residence, which was hard for women like Channah to find. She felt lucky to have arrived in Bremen still possessing her dignity and her spirit. Channah wanted so much to have a room of her own. What a wonderful thought. She was more hopeful that she could achieve having a home of her own. Jacob almost took all of her hopes and dreams. How could she have married him? What made a man turn his allegiance from his wife back to his mother? Can he forget all that they meant to each other? He wanted Channah as his slave. She must stop mentally torturing herself. She must stop thinking about Jacob.

# 6

# The Silver Spoons

Channah lay on the bed in her room in Rabbi Sheer's house. She paid one month's rent in advance for a bed, one meal per day, and two cups of tea. Why hadn't she thought to bring tea? The leaves would have fit into any pocket. She was not wise enough to bring a cup and saucer. The two large silver tablespoons and four forks fit in her carpetbag. She slept on her bag to keep her cutlery safe. Only if she became desperate would she trade them for money. Things would have to get pretty bad before she would resort to selling her silverware. They were silver utensils; this meant they were valuable.

The silver spoons were so beautiful. If only she could be comfortable using them. How could she keep them shiny if they were used? She couldn't stop thinking these were the only items she was awarded in her divorce from Jacob. This was not fair!

No one owned anything like these two large silver spoons. If she ran out of money, she could sell them. Who would buy them?

*Channah's silver forks and spoons.*

Several people she knew thought they were worthwhile to bring to America. They were the next best thing to gold, so popular that many jewelers invested in similar spoons. They became a cherished treasure to her. Channah didn't feel so poor with the silver flatware in her carpetbag. The spoons[8] were a consolation, a source of comfort. They were tradable.

Channah had these silver spoons and could have traded them for cash. They were silver utensils; this meant they had intrinsic value. These spoons were large enough, perhaps, for serving food. They were too large to eat with, but made great serving utensils. When they were utilized, they indicated the luxury to eat slowly.

---

[8] When I first saw them as a young girl in my grandmother's belongings, they were actually usable and they indicated a family of means. Now, I also use these spoons.

Their value was maximized. The silver spoons were a sign of wealth. Somehow, they were never lost or mislaid.

In the meantime, Channah at dinnertime in the boarding house set her own table with these large utensils. Her attempt at elegance was obvious. She didn't use them often for fear of attracting thieves. Somehow, they were never stolen—probably because Channah kept them with her always. Why did she keep them close to her? They became something to Channah like the Mycenaean cup that the famous Helen brought with her from Troy in 1200 B.C.

# 7

## Finding Work

Channah was afraid to run out of money and she had to find work. What could she do? She couldn't cook, couldn't sew, but she could create beautiful stained glass windows. This was not enough, she decided.

Women were not trained for a man's work. "You have eyes, what did you learn? You are not prepared to take care of children. You couldn't even have them. Barren! Barren! Barren!" she said to herself.

Channah thought about how she helped her father make stained glass and listened to the wonderful stories he told about building the tsar's cousin's windows. People always loved hearing his stories. Revan Spector's stained glass window designs were very much sought after.

Channah thought people would cherish stained glass in Germany too. This wasn't to be easy. She had brought nothing to show her talent. Channah racked her brain and easily remembered discussions she had with her father about his work. Not only did he work for one of the tsar's cousin, but he also repaired some of the stained glass windows in a chapel of the monastery that was built on the edge of a town near the city of Tbilisi. These stained glass windows were insignificant in size. They were purely for decoration and did not tell a story like the other windows Revan had designed.

Channah remembered that her father would sell berries to buy chemicals and cutting equipment along with dyes made from vegetables to make stained glass windows. In the process of creating the stained glass, Channah remembered her father using whatever natural resources he could find.

# 8

# *The Fox and the Grapes*

Channah often thought of her father and how she discussed the designs that he sold. Why couldn't she do the same work that her father did? Would the rabbi help her by letting her decorate the synagogue with her stained glass designs?

After much effort, Channah convinced the rabbi to let her have one window to decorate to embellish the synagogue.[9] Channah of Tbilisi was an unknown woman and a woman scorned for her inability to bear children. Designing a window was a difficult task, she thought. Could she do it? What story should her stained glass design tell? These windows often presented a theme or story, just as her father's windows did in Tbilisi. Channah thought this over and finally settled on the fable of the "Fox and the Grapes" by Aesop.

---

[9] The author is familiar with stained glass windows in her synagogue in Freehold, New Jersey, that were used to raise money for the maintenance of the synagogue.

*Example of Fox and Grapes stained glass window.*

Channah remembered her father's techniques for making stained glass using colors obtained from berries and vegetables. She also remembered how he would make different pieces of glass into specific shapes using a mold in a variety of colors. She marveled at her father's ability to satisfy the tsar's cousin with not just replacing broken stained glass windows, but with the insertion of new windows with new subjects.

The window that Channah designed would have a subject that was not offensive to the synagogue's congregation. Channah envisioned a beautiful stained glass design of a fox from the fable. She could hardly believe that she was trying to design a window for the synagogue that her father would have found a simple task.

How could a woman who was childless take on the most difficult job of creating a single stained glass window to decorate a synagogue in Bremen? The window would be placed to the left of the altar so natural light could come in from behind it. It could take one or even two years to finish a design, but Channah had to begin. Channah had to know the measurements of the window. She had to know if the window would be naturally lit from the exterior. She wished she had her father's tools, molds, and measuring equipment for the project. She decided the colors should suit the other colors in the building, especially the walls, chairs, and carpets. The walls were an off-white color.

The subject was easy. The window size was more important. She decided to make a two-by-four-foot window. It would be perfect next to the altar. She decided to place the window to the left of the *bema*, altar, and didn't want the colors and exterior light source to overwhelm the stained glass window and cast a strong a reflective light on the congregants.

Channah started to sketch the various components of the fox, the sky, the ground, and the grapes on a vine. Channah wanted to rewrite the fable so that the fox was successful in eating the grapes—just as she wished to be successful in conceiving a child one day. Channah listed the colors that she needed: brown, blue, red, orange, purple, yellow, and green. Where would Channah find the components to make the stained glass? She wished that she could go back to her father and ask him what to do.

Channah wondered why she couldn't just decorate a side window with stained glass. Perhaps one not directly in front of the congregation. Why couldn't there be a vote to decide the project?

Perhaps she could find fruits and vegetables in the market to use for staining the glass. Even rejected fruits and vegetables would do.

Channah repeatedly wished her father was there to discuss the subject and the installation and even the colors and design for her first stained glass window. She remembered how Revan explained that making a stained glass window was popular in religious buildings since the Middle Ages, from the twelfth to fifteenth centuries A.D.

Revan had learned the art of stained glass from his father, who had learned it from his father. But Channah, a woman who only helped her father with his work, would now replicate it in Bremen. This stained glass window would become famous, just as famous as Revan's work in Tbilisi.

# 9

## Installing the Window

The first opportunity to install the "Fox and the Grapes" window must be successful. If only Revan were there to oversee the process. She really could use his approval of her work. However, Channah herself knew the window looked magnificent.

The window would be hung next to the area where the cabinet containing the Torah was located. This cabinet could not be moved unless it was by someone who had permission from powerful official authority. Channah knew it would not interfere with the action of the installation of the stained glass window.

Channah thought, "Why didn't I make a Bible scene instead of a tale with an animal and fruit?" The rabbi was moved by the design, though. He selected passages in the Bible to support the simple design. He even talked about using it in an effort to bring his congregation together. This little *shul* was becoming known for Channah's design of the "Fox and the Grapes."

Channah did not have a camera to record[10] her stained window of "The Fox and the Grapes." She could only explain the design to her family and friends later on. Sometimes, she would even sketch the design from memory.

Channah made a few friends in the synagogue from her work. However, there was resentment that a woman succeeded in her goal and did work in the *shul*. When the window was ready for installation, the tale of "The Fox and the Grapes" bothered some people and pleased others. However, it mostly bothered the rabbi's wife. Channah heard this jealous woman constantly berating her husband.

But the rabbi saw the window's significance. It attracted people of all sorts to come and see the *shul*. What difference did it make that a devoted woman had done the job? A woman who was running away from something. A woman who kept to herself and ate with her large silver spoons at the dining room table.

During one mealtime, someone asked Channah when she would leave for America. Channah was shocked to hear the question just when she was prepared to install the stained glass window. Channah started to feel that she was some sort of threat to the *rebbetzin*, the rabbi's wife.

Channah, in her innocence, ignored the effect that others had on her. She was a single woman who ate alone with special silver spoons and forks—no knives, just spoons and forks. She worked carefully to put them away in her carpetbag. Channah carried the bag everywhere. At most, it weighed as much as a cocker spaniel. Channah was a strong, confident woman, though the bag started to bother her shoulders.

---

[10] Most ordinary people did not own cameras at this point; only professional photographers did.

The resentment from the synagogue's female members for Channah's stained glass window started to make life miserable for her. Sometimes she wondered if she should have stayed in Georgia. However, how could she ever think that she could have lived in the same community as Jacob for another five minutes? He was in no way supportive. He chose to let her live a disgraced life.

As soon as the *ghet* was completed, Jacob let it be known that not only was he already looking for a new wife, but also that it was imperative for him to find one and get her pregnant quickly. He had no consideration for Channah's feelings and certainly no understanding of the mortification she experienced. This was the man she loved and cherished? What a mistake she made marrying him.

Channah had wished that she could go home to her parents' house in Georgia and try to live a normal life, but it was impossible. Channah had to stay in Bremen and never return to Tbilisi again.

Channah's sister Sophie, always determined and an independent thinker, made the choice to leave for America on her own. Sophie was several years younger than Channah. Channah missed Sophie's cooking, primarily her baking. Sophie's *schnecken* were magical. If Channah was at all sad, a few of Sophie's *schnecken* would always make her feel better. Sophie became famous for her mood-changing little cakes. Channah often thought of them when she was down and suddenly, like a miracle, she would get happy. She never tried to cook them. Sophie's *schnecken* were like a drug. There would be no comparison with Sophie's cooking. People would just laugh.

Channah took little care of herself. This was what Channah wanted. She felt like she needed a home like she had with Jacob. But all she had was a room in the rabbi's house. Undoubtedly, the rabbi's wife was threatened by her presence. Channah would not last long in this living arrangement. She would either have to move out or leave for America. Channah knew that the only solution was to go to America, which also meant she had to give up any hope of ever seeing her parents again.

She had to make her arrangements. Her little job for the synagogue brought her just enough money to buy her ticket on the Red Star Line to Philadelphia. Channah knew she must purchase her passage for the ship soon.

If things went well, within the year she could be in Philadelphia with her sister. She knew her job at the synagogue in Bremen would be over. They had no more stained glass windows to build and the congregation was furious that they had to pay her. It was silly to think that she could make a living making stained glass windows.

Channah found the office for the Red Star Line, where she learned the price of the ticket and the ship's departure schedule. She decided she would have her own room on the boat rather than stay in steerage. As her only source of income had been making the stained glass window, she would use most of her savings. The remaining money would come from selling the forks and spoons. This was out of the question, though. There was a ship leaving in two weeks for America. There would be no remorse about leaving Bremen.

While in Bremen, Channah realized that she made the right move. Her only mistake was not taking her tools to make stained glass windows.

# 10

## *Ticket to America*

As planned, Channah got her passage to America. On her way to the docks, she walked through different neighborhoods, her belongings held close in her carpetbag. Channah felt strong and determined to get herself on the ship. No one bothered her as her simple clothing didn't look too costly and there was no sign of jewelry except her gold wedding band. She appeared to lack sophistication. The Red Star Line would make only one stop in Liverpool, then go on to America.

Though she had been in Bremen for nearly a year, the time seemed to have passed quickly. She heard very little from her parents. The postcard she sent to them in Yiddish must have gone missing. After all, didn't she tell the rabbi's brother when he went to Tbilisi to hand the postcard personally to her parents and report her well-being in Bremen and tell of her stained glass window in the *shul?*

Channah hoped her father would be proud of the stained glass window. Maybe she could draw a picture of the window for him. She would refrain from mentioning the resentment she had felt, the ill will from the synagogue members that had pushed her to America.

# 11

## The Voyage to Philadelphia

"Will the rocking ever stop?" Channah thought as she made her way across the Atlantic Ocean. Some people sailed first-class. Channah didn't want to spend the money, but she wanted her own room. She always wanted her own room. "What for?" she questioned herself. To keep her privacy? Maybe she would do better on deck and run to the railings when the seas became too rough.

Food was no issue. If she ate, then she didn't get sick. The meals mainly consisted of potatoes with some kind of meat. Ironically, they never ate fish even though they were at sea. Passengers were also served stew and soup. It was pretty much the same thing every day, plenty of bread, never cake, and sometimes apples or bananas. "Is that a banana?" someone would yell excitedly.

Philadelphia was coming into sight. Channah was getting excited. She never believed that she would make it to America. It wouldn't be long until she saw her sister, Sophie. Channah tried to contain herself. Euphoric didn't begin to describe how Channah felt. She didn't know if her postcards with her arrival information had reached Sophie. Would someone meet her at the port? Was Sophie's address correct? Did people read her cards? Channah wrote in Yiddish, but her cursive looked like chicken scratch. She hoped that someone was waiting for her.

Channah couldn't wait to see Sophie and eat her *schnecken*. She knew that Sophie was married to a nice man named Max Pomerantz. Sophie loved him dearly. He was tall and kind and responsibly worked five days a week as a house painter. Sophie was well taken care of and comfortable, but hardly wealthy.

Channah was happy for Sophie, but knew this journey was especially tedious and time-consuming for both women. Channah couldn't imagine how Sophie came to America by herself—and by choice.

Channah realized early on that in America, she must learn to read English. This was America. There were no signs written in Yiddish. Channah was greatly troubled by her linguistic limitation, unable to read or speak any English. She was not alone in this deficiency. The first thing Sophie did upon her arrival to America was to go to school and learn to read and speak English.

# 12

## Unpacking

Channah was now enjoying her good fortune. She sat at a table in Sophie's kitchen and enjoyed a glass of tea with a spoon of strawberry jam. There wasn't a *schnecken* in sight. Being with Sophie was the moment she had dreamt about since she left Georgia.

She had finally found her sister Sophie in America. Sophie and Max had a little house painted by Max from top to bottom with the leftover paint from his jobs.

Sophie had placed Channah in a room of her own. Channah immediately opened her bag and took out the beautiful pillow-cases that she had hand embroidered. Optimistically, she included a second pillowcase that matched the house. The second pillow-case she carried would have been for a spouse. She did not care. God had already been too good to her. She was in America, settled in with her younger sister.

"Let's send a postcard to our parents to tell them we are well and together," Channah suggested to Sophie.

Max had been to the store and purchased some food: a chicken, still alive; a kilo of beef; and maybe a few pounds of short ribs. Sophie knew what to do with these peculiar ingredients. Everything could be cooked. They watched the chicken run around the small backyard. The family cat perched itself on the wall and the chicken started to flutter, afraid that the cat would attack.

# 13

## Sophie's House

People came and went from Sophie's house. Channah loved her room on the second floor. She was finally by herself. Was this finally the room of her dreams? Probably not. "Let's see what happens," she said when asked if she would stay.

Everyone heard that Channah was from the old country and wanted to see her to find out who still lived in Georgia. The young girls tried to understand why she left home, if it was so great there. They said, "*Gedenk,* remember how we used to see such beautiful mountains and even a beautiful sea? Georgia is so beautiful."

The girls asked, "If it is so beautiful, why did everyone leave everything and come here to our dirty streets now worse with only buildings on either side? There are no gardens in America and very few trees." Sophie had one tree out front, around which little flowers and ferns grew. There was another tree with large leaves in her small garden. They all marveled at Sophie's red brick row house with large windows facing the street.

The first floor had a strong layout. It was nothing at all like her parents' home in Georgia. A beautiful armoire sat in Sophie's bedroom at the front overlooking the street, which led to the living room, then back to the dining room and ended with the kitchen all the way in the back of the house. Down a long hallway was a staircase that led to the second floor where there were four bedrooms that she would rent out to students, each with an armoire to make up for the lack of closet space.

Channah couldn't imagine herself in a home like Sophie's forever. She often thought of her home in Tbilisi with Jacob.

Sophie's house was dark. Channah realized that shutting off the lights was the equivalent to blowing out the candles. There was hardly any natural light because there were only windows in the front and the back of the house. It would take a few years until electricity would be available for every house. For now, candles and fireplaces would do.

Electricity for the whole city was not a simple matter. Electrifying entire buildings, like the Wanamaker Building,[11] was a dangerous procedure. The lit-up building frightened people who were unfamiliar with such a glow in the evening. It seemed dangerous. However, it was surprisingly cheap to install.

When Channah was settled into Sophie's home in Philadelphia, the sisters received a letter from Georgia announcing that their mother, Nessa, would come to visit them. Revan was unable to make the trip.

During their mother's visit, they shopped in Wanamaker's Department Store for gifts to bring back to Georgia. She went back to Georgia and returned to her husband, the stained glass artisan.

---

[11] Thomas Edison wired the Wanamaker Building and the neighboring residents complained of the glare. He probably used knob-and-tube wiring or copper wiring with rubber insulation.

Channah's little sister, Rachel, would never come to America.[12] If she had come to America, she and her family would have been able to escape the pogroms. Channah would have been so happy to see her baby sister.

---

[12] She would remain to be murdered by the end of the pogroms in Georgia. Pogroms were anti-Jewish rioting and slaughters begun in the nineteenth century. As late as 1939, a Russian was overheard saying in Philadelphia, "In Russia, I kill a Jew for 10 cents." Killing Jews and pogroms in general were considered crimes at this time.

# 14

## Harris Pomerantz

Channah could not believe the good fortune she had living with Sophie in Philadelphia. Her fortune was about to change again. This time she was not prepared for it.

Channah looked tall and leggy with long auburn hair in the latest American style. Her hair was swept off her forehead, peeled back at the top of her head and puffed out at the sides and forehead. It looked shiny, especially now that she could wash her hair with rainwater, which she collected in a pail in her sister's little garden. She hardly thought of Georgia, except when she wondered about her parents.

Channah counted her blessings. This time she mustn't look for things to worry about. Did she have any money left? Channah sat on her bed and shook out her large carpetbag into her lap. What she was looking for, or listening for, was the sound of coins jingling. Paper money doesn't make much noise. She heard nothing. Why didn't she check earlier?

Then she heard a brief clinking sound. She knew this noise and she grabbed for the silver spoons before they rolled off the bed onto the hook rug. Channah had bought the rug to avoid putting her bare feet on the gray-painted wide slats of the floor.

She didn't have hardwood floors in her parents' home in Georgia, which had pounded earth floors that needed to be cleaned by a feather broom. Sophie's floor was painted gray by Max and had wide boards with pronounced joints. For the less affluent, carpentry in America was a hurried job, not carefully executed by skilled carpenters.

Channah put all her possessions together. She had not done this since she prepared for her trip from Georgia to Bremen. Now she was finally in Philadelphia with her sister and in her own room in Sophie's house.

Why wait to enjoy these? Life had been difficult ever since she left her parents' house and stopped working with her father. Her success in Bremen with the *shul's* stained glass was disappointing. She now recognized that her poor reception within the Jewish community was because she instigated jealousy as a woman, because she took work and pay from men.

Her possessions did not make her very happy, but her professional success with the stained glass window gave her an air of confidence. She could now be considered a professional stained glass artisan.

It was her perception of confidence that impressed Harris Pomerantz, who had come to visit with his nephew, Max Pomerantz, to discuss a paint job on the train cars Harris owned as a result of winning a card game. His opponent had little cash and offered the empty train cars to pay his debt for the game. Harris was surprised at his good fortune. He now had a solution to a problem that haunted him. He was happy to have won these trains

*Harris Pomerantz,
Helen's grandfather and
father of Beatrice.*

because it provided a place for him to store the scrap metal he sold. He could now consolidate the metal rather than keep it in a variety of barns.

What could Harris do? They were his only offer and a win is a win. His brother, Amen, also acquired a very important property in the same game. Amen won the option to lease a lot at 1525 Chestnut Street in Philadelphia for just one dollar. Amen owned a stationery store down the block and was content with its location. This was often the way immigrants in America made their success, by wagering what they already owned.

"What are you going to do with this land?" Harris asked Amen.

"I'm going to build a store on it!"

"What are you going to sell? That is no place to sell food or garments. It is near many offices."

Amen took time to think about what he would sell in his shop. He decided to move his stationery and office supplies store and sell products to the nearby offices. "Harris, why don't you be my partner?" Amen asked. "We can sell your trains and buy a stock of stationary."

Harris shrugged and said, "I can't share the small profits that we make off the sale of a few sheets of paper."

Harris had no foresight for Amen's business, which he set up in the most advanced manner equipped with a fine printing press. After all, isn't this what Benjamin Franklin did? Not quite. He wrote the works that he printed. Amen just sold paper and printing supplies.

"Your business is not for me. I don't want to make pennies at a time," said Harris.

This was the same Harris Pomerantz who came to call at Sophie and Max's home looking for a painter to letter the name of his company on the trains that he had won. The cars were stationed on the tracks near the Delaware River.

# 15

## The Courting of Channah

Harris was outside Max's red brick row house. He knocked and Channah answered the door. He did not expect such an attractive woman to open the door. The woman greeted Harris at the door wearing a sophisticated black shawl. The sight of Channah at the doorway shook Harris to his core.

Harris found his long-retired charm and quickly put it to use on Channah. She was such a beautiful and tall woman that he couldn't help but want to impress her.

Who is this man who looks like he came straight out of the barbershop? Channah wondered.

"*Was ist seine namen?*" Channah asked. Who are you?

"Harris Pomerantz," was his response.

Harris's wife had died three years earlier, leaving him alone with six children: five girls and a boy. Channah had heard this bit of information from Max. She also heard that Harris was now looking for someone to take care of his children.

Channah, a woman called barren, found herself hoping for Harris's approval. Harris was at a loss for words, maybe because of Channah's good looks, her age, and her polite demeanor. Harris and Channah were immediately comfortable with one another.

"Would you like to go for a ride in my carriage?" Harris asked Channah. "Grab a hat and we will go for a ride." This was the only thing Harris thought to say at that moment completely forgetting his reason for stopping by the house. "My carriage is parked on the street, why not take advantage of it?"

"I have to tell Sophie first."

"Is Sophie your mother?" Harris asked.

*Was wills du? Ich will du namen* for a ride. What do you want? I want to take you for a ride. Channah turned away and ran to the kitchen. "Harris wants to take me in his carriage. Do I have to wear a hat?" Channah asked Sophie. "Tell me that you have a beautiful hat." Sophie didn't have one for her.

"I'll go with you, but I can't go out without a hat," Channah said to Harris. When Harris heard this delightful response, he promised to take her to a millinery shop to find her a beautiful hat. This is a harmless request.

"I will go to a millinery shop, and then we will take my carriage to Fairmount Park," Harris told Channah.

Harris told Channah his plan and she became confused. Can she go? Is this an engagement? If a man buys a woman a hat, is this an informal engagement? She did not know the protocol for courting in America.

It was not an engagement but a courting event. Whatever it was, Channah liked the idea of going out with Harris.

Channah wanted to cry. This was too much, too fast for her. This was a new culture and she didn't know if she liked it. Was this how people were courted in America?

Harris saw Channah was nonplussed. He thought, "Does she want more? Must I buy her a ring? Will this scare her? There are no parents to ask permission, just Sophie and her husband, my nephew. Maybe I need a rabbi. Am I making a marriage proposal? Do I just want to possess her?"

Harris stopped and thought, "I'm rushing this. However, Channah would be a wonderful addition to my family and would take good care of my children. If I want this, I have to do it properly: buy her a ring and everything."

Channah did not know American customs. All she did was say hello to Max's uncle. Now she was getting married. "All I own are two pillowcases and some silver spoons. God help me," she thought. She had no means to offer a dowry to Harris unless he liked silver spoons and forks.

Harris was carried away by the situation and overcome by her beauty.

Harris left to buy Channah a hat. "She is so beautiful and strong. She will make a wonderful wife and mother to my six children," he thought. "I must tell the children about Channah; that she will soon be their mother and live with us at 4th and Spruce Street."

Channah knew nothing about Harris except that he was very handsome, not tall, and would provide anything she needed. She did not know how she could help him with the children, though.

"Marrying without a formal proposal is considered immoral," Channah thought. Harris was familiar with this regulation in America and proceeded anyhow.

Harris returned with a hatbox and the rings, driving the carriage pretty fast through the neighborhood. A forthcoming proposal of marriage energized him.

Channah was shocked to see Harris driving his carriage up to Sophie's house again. Channah was even more shocked to see

Harris take a man out of the back seat. The old man was bearded and wore a yarmulka.[13]

Channah heard Yiddish spoken between Harris and the taller old man, a rabbi. She heard *chusunah,* a wedding. If you needed a rabbi for a ceremony, go to the nearest *shul.*

Channah was being swept off her feet. "Harris is so handsome," she later told her sister. "Maybe it would do me good to marry again. First, I want to meet the children. They need a mother."

---

[13]  A yarmulka is a skullcap worn by Jewish men.

# 16

## The Proposal

Sophie's house was almost out of the city and to the north. Harris's house was in the heart of Philadelphia on 4th and Spruce Streets, near Mikveh Israel synagogue and the Jewish cemetery.

Channah was swept off her feet by Harris. He had a handsome face, decorated with a reddish beard, and was about fifty years old. Channah was almost breathless and was now a willing model for the Gibson Girl[14] hat that Harris had bought her. The hat gave Channah such height that Harris chuckled at the sight of such a giant woman. She was so kind and understanding of his plight as a widower and his poor children motherless at such a young age.

Harris, the fervent almost-fiancé of Channah, was determined to attach himself by marriage to this goddess of a woman. He

---

[14] The Gibson Girl was considered the ideal look for women in the late nineteenth and early twentieth centuries as portrayed by the drawings of Charles Dana Gibson.

planned to dramatically give her a ring with a one-carat diamond and a matching gold wedding band.

Harris retrieved his carriage from the shed, the nearest shed to his house on Spruce Street. He intended to show Channah his house. He reviewed what he accomplished in regards to Channah. Most importantly, he decided he needed to make her a formal proposal of marriage. Harris was in charge of his house with all his children and his former wife's parents. The situation would change when Harris married Channah.

When Harris announced he was going to marry again, his family was upset to hear this. "Who is this Gibson Girl?" they asked each other.

"She is in the carriage," Harris answered. "I have not really asked her yet." The children ran to the window and saw a tall woman standing near the horse that pulled the carriage, calming the animal down. The animal was lathered up from the grand tour that Harris had given Channah.

Harris started to make arrangements for the wedding.

He was so serious that he proposed marriage to Channah after just one trip to Fairmount Park.[15] Then he showed her his home on Spruce Street where they would live as husband and wife.

Channah was delighted to marry Harris. Hopefully, she would have children of her own and no longer be called barren. She longed for a child of her own. Was she too old? Harris didn't mind her age, especially because he didn't want any more children, and thought that Channah was too old to get pregnant.

---

[15] Fairmount Park was designed by Robert Morris Copeland in 1812. At 2,2052 acres, it is the largest park in Philadelphia.

"Will we change after we are married?" Channah pondered. She rarely thought of Jacob, but she had wondered if he ever thought of her.

# 17

## Stained Glass in Philadelphia

Channah thought of her father's stained glass business and especially of her work in Bremen. Could she find an outlet to further her skill in Philadelphia? Who could she ask? No one she knew was familiar with stained glass. Only some of the Christian churches, like the one on 18th and Spruce Streets, permitted such decoration in the windows.

When Channah asked Harris to stop when driving the carriage so she could see the stained glass up close, he drove faster not understanding. Channah could not tell him about Bremen and the window with "The Fox and the Grapes."

"In the Mikveh *shul*, they may have this stained glass that you are anxious to see," Harris said. "Why do you always ask to see a stained glass window?"

Channah told Harris that her father made such windows in the churches in Tbilisi. She tried to tell him about the *shul* in Bremen and how she decorated a stained glass window with Aesop's "The

Fox and the Grapes," but he didn't want to hear about it. This amazed Channah, but she was told that Americans were very busy making money and they didn't care about art or decorations. So, she decided to stay quiet about herself. Instead, she asked Harris about his business in scrap metal.

This confused him. Women weren't supposed to think about business. Channah was different. She had to earn her own money. How could she explain this to him? All the money she had ever earned was from the stained glass window she installed in Bremen.

# 18

## *Carriage Rides with Harris*

On one of Channah and Harris's carriage rides, Channah noticed that in America, maybe only in Philadelphia, the houses near the waterfront were used by sea captains' families. They could be built quickly and sold just as fast. Channah knew that in Bremen she never saw any little brick houses with shutters painted white.

As Channah was driven west down Spruce Street, the facades changed and the houses grew taller. The windows were also different in size. The homes then changed from red brick to brownstone as they continued west. Many of the houses had little porticos, some with columns, especially ionic. These appealed to Channah, and she imagined herself wearing a billowing dress while entering this kind of house.

The dreaming had to stop. She must give Harris some attention, which she was happy to do. He was a fascinating man and so

*Portico Row on Spruce Street in Philadelphia.*

handsome with that precisely trimmed beard. "I must appreciate his interest in me," Channah thought.

Harris had been driving his two-horse carriage down Spruce Street and needed time to visit his brother, Amen. He made a sharp turn on 16th Street and drove over to Chestnut Street.

One thing that Channah did notice was how narrow the streets were. They were just wide enough for two carriages to turn at one time. Parking was difficult. Harris arrived at Amen's lot at 1525 Chestnut Street. However, there was too much traffic. He could drive by or stop on the corner of 16th and Chestnut Streets, get out, and walk back to Amen's lot. He decided to do the latter.

Harris said, "Amen has just leased this lot after he returned from traveling and he is using another building at 34 South 15th

Street until he has finished constructing the new one. He has architects, Simon and Bassett, designing it. I think he is competing with McArthur's City Hall,[16] which was finished in 1901."

However, it would be almost impossible to compete with the massive size of Philadelphia City Hall. Its north tower was so important and grand that on a clear day the clock on it could be seen from forty miles away. The building was further embellished with a statue of William Penn designed by Alexander Calder. It stood at thirty-seven feet tall on top of the 587-foot tower, and watched over Philadelphia.

Channah was overwhelmed with all that she saw. "It is really enough for today," she said to Harris. "*Gnug, wir muss zur haus gehen.*" We must return to Sophie's house.

This time, Harris realized that his driving had been too much for Channah. She didn't have a clue about the layout of the city and where she had been. Harris knew he hadn't explained the way William Penn designed the city into four squares and a grid. He would save that for another time.

Channah was getting hungry for a meal. How could she tell Harris? Should they go back to Sophie's house? She couldn't wait. Channah dreamt of homemade soup or stew. She had heard about Marshall Street and thought maybe if she said the street name, he would understand her plight.

"Marshall Street. *Wie ist es?*" Harris was shocked to hear her say the name of the shopping district for Jews. This collection of shops and carts did not suit his elegant carriage. He wondered why she wanted to go there. Then he realized that she must be hungry.

---

[16] The architects who designed Philadelphia City Hall are John McArthur Jr. and Thomas Ustick Walter. The exterior is made from marble, granite, and limestone. Thomas Ustick Walter also designed the homes on Portico Row, as well as Girard College for Orphans.

*City Hall in Philadelphia.*

"Are you hungry? Would you like to get lunch?" Harris asked.

Channah was embarrassed to say yes, but a piece of bread and a cut of cheese would be perfection.

Channah had no idea of a good lunch location. That explained why she wanted to go home to Sophie's. Sophie's icebox was full of delicious foods of all kinds. Sophie had also recently baked a fresh batch of *schnecken.*

"*Zie ist hungarich.* She is hungry. Why didn't I ask her? Of course, she wants to go home to Sophie's. Sophie is the most wonderful cook. *A gluz te und a kietchel,* a glass of tea and a cookie, would be just great," Harris thought.

"Maybe Wanamaker's has a place for tea?" Harris said to himself. Of course, they could go to the Crystal Tea Room[17] in the Wanamaker building.

Channah may find the department store too big to shop in easily and the dining room too fancy, but the escalators would be fun and different than in Bremen.

The escalators and electricity were frightening to some people. "Let's go to Wanamaker's for tea," Harris suggested.

Harris was so smitten with Channah that he treated her with spectacular charm. He was a true gentleman hoping to impress Channah. Channah wondered again if it was possible that they could get married soon. Channah was surprised at how her feelings for Harris developed so soon after acquiring the *ghet* from Jacob.

After such an awful first marriage, Channah couldn't believe that she wanted to get married yet again. She trusted that Harris would make a nice husband because she saw how he treated his children and in-laws with such great consideration.

---

[17] The Crystal Tea Room is located on the eighth floor of the Wanamaker Building. It opened in 1911.

# 19

## The Wedding

"Channah," Harris said, "Why wait any longer to get married?" Harris was persuasive. Channah started to like the idea of marrying Harris. She started to call him Harry when they were alone. But more often, she called him Mr. Pomerantz.

"Sophie, Harry wants to take me shopping for rings. He wants to buy an engagement ring with a diamond," Channah said. She was overwhelmed by his amorous behavior. "We are going to Jewelers' Row. One of Harry's friends specializes in diamonds."

Wearing her hat, Channah went to the jewelers to pick out an engagement ring and wedding band. "Harry, you know so much about these marriage customs," she said. Channah didn't need an engagement ring; she was comfortable with just the affirmation that they were getting married.

Channah still felt a little uncomfortable with Harris. There was not a lot of expression of love from him. He was not affectionate, and hardly an ardent lover, but he did what was expected of him.

Channah was excited to go shopping for the rings. "Channah, do you have any documentation of your *ghet* in Georgia?" Harris asked her.

Finally, Channah had time to think about what she got herself into. A new marriage to a man she knew little about. Channah wondered why she was jumping into the marriage so quickly.

Channah said to Harris, "I want another hat when we wed. When we get married, we must have rings and a white hat with a scarf, and if possible, have a wedding picture taken. I want to send it to my parents and tell them that we got married. I'm scared to make a sacred commitment to you."

Harris said, "*Was willst du ich leibe du*. What do you want? I love you."

"Should we go first to the rabbi?" Channah asked.

Harris replied, "No, first we must go to City Hall."

Channah said to Harris, "Where will we live? Will we live in your house on Spruce Street?"

He must tell his family that he was going to marry Channah. His house at 4th and Spruce was still occupied by his children and his in-laws.

Channah had to go to Wanamaker's. The hat department was on the first floor. Channah quickly purchased two hats. Harris paid for them, but he did not want to see the wedding hat until they went to the rabbi for the ceremony. Channah now owned three hats.

Channah put on the Gibson Girl hat. The hat had a large brim and lots of ruffled fabric and large plumes. Channah felt very elegant. Harris was proud of her. They went to City Hall to get a marriage license.

They must go back to Sansom Street to buy the rings they had chosen. Harris remembered that he still had the rings from his first wedding. He bought them from a jeweler on 7th and Sansom Streets, the same store where he would buy Channah's rings.

When his first wife died, Harris gave her rings to their oldest daughter, Lilly. The wedding bands were removed from his wife's hand before she was buried.

When Channah went to the jewelry store, the jewelers said to Harris, "This woman is so beautiful. How did you get a beauty like her?"

Harris was very proud of his idea to marry Channah and planned to move her into his house within the next few days. The wedding ceremony would be beautiful and Sophie would prepare dinner for them. None of their relatives except Sophie and Max knew about the upcoming marriage plans.

Channah didn't know whether she should cry or laugh. These events were a shock and a surprise to this Gibson Girl who had struggled so hard to get to America. The crying didn't last long. Her laughing turned into a tight smile, almost like the Mona Lisa. Channah had a secret, though. Her secret was that she already loved Harris.

# 20

## Moving into Harris's House

After the marriage ceremony at City Hall and dinner at Sophie's house, Channah moved what little she owned into Harris's house. She told Harris that she preferred that their bedroom be on the second floor.

Channah thought back to Georgia and remembered that she never had to climb stairs to get to her bedroom. No one in her family would believe in such an inconvenience or the luxury of such a large house.

Philadelphia houses were logically constructed and designed for family use, in this case. The rooms were stacked with the servants' quarters on the top floor and the kitchen in the basement with a set of stairs for use from the service quarters to the kitchen. Some houses, Channah learned, had a separate building for carriages and servants. Delancey, Spruce, and Panama Streets were where the stables for the horses and carriages were kept; even the stables were built with a second floor.

Channah was not used to the spread-out arrangement of Harris's house.

After spending a week getting used to Harris's home, she became tired. The kitchen and laundry were in the basement. The first floor had the living room, dining room, parlor, Harris's study, and office. The second floor had the master bedroom and dressing rooms. The third floor was for the children and their pets. The fourth floor was for boarders; one of these boarders was a beautiful actress who had moved in just after Channah and Harris got married. One could also reach the guest room by the servant stairs that started in the basement kitchen behind the stove. The fifth floor was for the servants of the house.

# 21

## Channah's New Family

Lilly, Minnie, Esther, Ernest, Frieda, and Francis. So many children, so quick. Channah, on first arrival, liked the children. Each rattled off his or her name quickly and marveled at their very tall new mother. Channah tried her best to remember their names. However, the one boy, Ernest, seemed somewhat lost with the five girls surrounding him.

The six children had to be organized according to their various activities and schedules. The children were difficult to understand and were as much a puzzle to Channah as Harris was.

They spoke only English and Channah knew only Yiddish. The children all spoke beautifully as a result of their fine education and some tough teachers who put their heart and soul into teaching them. The children attended the newly opened General George A. McCall School just two blocks away from the house.

The first time Channah was in her and Harris's bedroom, she saw that all she had to fill was one chest of drawers. They were convenient. Fortunately, there were two armoires. There were no closets. One armoire seemed to be where Harris kept his suits, and the other would be for her two dresses.

Channah needed another dress for the synagogue and an additional dress for family events. Her only chance for variety and color were the pretty belts and silver jewelry that she brought from her home in Georgia.

Ten aprons were also put in her chest of drawers. They were stacked and embroidered so Channah did not look like the cleaning lady. In fact, these aprons were what caught Harris's eye. They also were embroidered at the waist in a charming kind of way.

Channah, now married to Harris, lived on Spruce Street in Harris's house with his children. Channah could remember the whirlwind courtship, like the rides in Harris's carriage and the wonderful dinners at the Bellevue Stratford Hotel.

She especially liked his carriage with lanterns on either side, which lit up at night. It was very romantic. Her previous experience with a lantern was when her ex-husband held one to her face when she was ill with smallpox. However, Harris did not keep up with the courtship for long.

Despite Channah's effort to provide his children with the air of a home, her methods were too old fashioned for them. Channah was not sophisticated and still a traditional old-country girl. Harris was no longer charmed by her Gibson Girl style, which had originally attracted him to Channah. The only thing he still liked was that she stood taller than he and couldn't be missed when she walked into a room.

There was nothing Channah could do to bring Harris home for dinner. He always said he was expecting a delivery of scrap metal and had to wait for it at the dock. Channah was afraid to check on him. Subconsciously, she didn't want to confront the truth as to why he wasn't coming home.

The few times Harris joined them, they ate around a large dining table, even the children. Now even some boarders were included and they all enjoyed meals prepared by Channah.

# 22

## Betrayal

On Camac Street, which was paved with wooden oak blocks, stood the Charlotte Cushman Club, a building that housed some actresses. It was just a few streets from Harris's home, and he became involved with one of the actresses who lived at the Charlotte Cushman Club. He met her after attending a play at the Walnut Street Theater.[18] Very soon, the woman moved to the fourth floor of Harris's home as a boarder.

Channah was appalled that Harris had found an actress more attractive than she. What was she to do? This had been another defeat for Channah. It was hard to explain, but after discussing his new folly, she tried to talk to her sister, Sophie, about another matter. Channah mentioned that she hadn't been feeling well lately, especially in the mornings. Sophie only said, "I think you're pregnant. Do not leave Harris. You won't be able to manage alone."

---

[18] The Walnut Street Theater opened in 1809 and is the oldest running theater in the United States.

However, every night Channah heard Harris go up to the fourth floor of their house. His excuse was to regulate the heat, but Channah knew differently.

She thought it was impossible that Harris didn't love her anymore.

Her final rejection came when Harris did not return to their room. Despondent was the word she would use to describe herself.

For a woman who did not like to cook, Channah tried very hard to make an exceptionally nice dinner. She produced, with a little help, a Georgian specialty with lots of eggplant and tomatoes with expensive lamb and fresh garlic.

Channah had decorated the room with scented candles and beautiful curtains, the latest newspapers, and a special copy of the *Daily Jewish Forward* with the latest news from Lithuania. Harris knew nothing about Lithuania, the intellectual capital of the Jews.

He ate his dinner and ran away like a boy going out to play. Harris did not even make a pretense of lingering. Channah could tell it was Harris's footsteps climbing up to the fourth floor. Channah was horrified. Harris did not even pretend that all was well. Harris did not want to pretend anymore.

Channah was pregnant. She knew that her body felt differently, like nothing she ever felt before. She had not menstruated in two or three months. What she had wanted for most of her forty-two years had finally happened. She knew that she was going to have a baby.

She wouldn't be considered barren anymore. Something wonderful was happening to her. Harris did not even suspect that she was pregnant.

Channah said to herself, "I think that our marriage is over. I can only go to Sophie. I'll go in the morning. I have to rest now. I have some money to take care of myself and certainly I'll do nothing else for Harris."

"Why am I not crying?" Channah said to herself, "Because I'm not to be described as barren anymore."

# 23

## *Leaving*

"Sophie, I'm going to be a mother."

Sophie rushed to put her arms around Channah. Sophie was younger and shorter than Channah, but today she felt like Channah's big sister or even her mother.

Sophie knew how much Channah suffered from the humiliation of being called barren. Channah had suffered since the *ghet* in Georgia and now, at forty-two years old, she was pregnant.

Sophie was not entirely pleased because she learned from Channah that Harris was sleeping with one of their boarders right under Channah's nose. Not all men were disgusting, but Channah seemed to have met up with most of them.

Sophie congratulated Channah and inquired about how she felt. She asked, "Does Harris know yet?"

However, Sophie knew it didn't matter to Channah one way or the other. Sophie asked Channah, "What are you going to do?"

Channah said, "I'm going to be the happiest mother ever. I want this child all to myself. I will not share the baby with Harris. He does not deserve one smile from its beautiful face. Sophie, I am leaving Harris tomorrow evening. Will you help me to pack up the few items I have? Can I beg you to let me stay at your house?"

Sophie couldn't contain her joy and she knew that Max, her husband, would do his best to make Channah feel welcomed. She was not certain that Max and Harris even got along.

Channah didn't cry about the failure of her second marriage. The overwhelming joy of potential motherhood gave her new strength and determination.

After another night of restlessness, Channah woke up ready to pack up all of her belongings in her chest and armoire.

Sophie and Max arrived early, as arranged, and ready to help Channah move. There was no overt sadness—just the dislike for Harris and the hope that he wouldn't return while they were moving.

No tears, no notes of explanation, just a quick disappearance. How was it possible that she was four months pregnant? Miracle of miracles. Even the little morning sickness was just a welcome component of Channah's condition.

Nothing was said to Channah about going to a doctor. She knew there was a different kind of joy. They all felt joy for Channah. There was all the love needed to support Channah's choice to go through this alone.

Channah said she needed only Sophie and Max. Harris had done his job. Channah often wondered why Harris didn't want to marry a younger woman and chose her instead. He probably thought Channah would never get pregnant because she was supposedly barren and middle aged. Harris already had six children and didn't want anymore. Getting Channah pregnant hadn't seemed possible!

# 24

## *Independent*

After Channah left her husband, Amen told Harris, "Channah seems happier now that she is pregnant. She doesn't seem to need you except for the money you owe her now that she has moved out of your house."

Channah was humiliated to hear this. Channah feared that she hadn't made Harris feel special enough. He had humiliated her with his affair with the boarder upstairs already. Channah had no choice but to leave.

It turned out that as soon as she was pregnant, she could do without Harris. Soon, she knew that she would no longer be referred to as barren. In fact, to this end, she and Harris were shocked by her pregnancy. Harris had thought, "She couldn't possibly get pregnant and would be the perfect wife to take care of my six motherless children." Channah had other plans. "She couldn't possibly conceive in her older age," Harris also thought.

Channah wanted a baby so much that nature worked in her favor. The baby would belong only to her. Harris recognized this and left her right away for someone who would make him feel special. That's why he continued to run up to the fourth-floor boarder.

Harris knew he loved the talented Channah, the wonderful designer of stained glass windows at home in Georgia and for the *shul* in Bremen. Anywhere that needed her designs, Channah would be there to make the stained glass.

How could Harris settle down to the point where he was a reliable husband? He couldn't. That's only possible when you're young and with your first wife. Now that he would be a father again under different circumstances, he couldn't give Channah the love that she needed. Her first thought was that he was too old. What happened to their wonderful romance in Fairmount Park?

Harris stayed home a few times to enjoy his children but he didn't know what to feed them. Harris didn't want another baby. His boy, Ernest, was his favorite, and they did everything together—especially business.

# 25

## The Baby

No matter Channah's age, her powerful body was called to action. Channah quickly settled in with Sophie and Max and allowed her baby to grow. It was almost a luxury for Channah. She was told frequently, "This is the time to take excellent care of yourself and the growing baby inside of you."

The women Channah knew did not share maternity clothes, but Channah needed to be comfortable and have loose fitting clothing. Channah, now five months pregnant, started knitting clothes for the baby. She had the special glow of a pregnant woman and enjoyed every minute of it. When she started to feel the baby move, she became ecstatic.

Sophie recommended that Channah find a doctor. This was America and medicine was different here. Somehow, Channah found herself a doctor—and surprisingly, a woman doctor.

Food also was not an issue with Channah. She started to take Sophie's advice on what and how much to eat. Sophie cooked and the two sisters both ate. Sophie gained a lot of weight and concealed chuckles when Channah barely showed her condition.

However, the happy look on Channah's face was good enough. There was no fear or anxiety, just wonderful anticipation and excitement for her "little expectant tulip." Somehow, Channah managed to always look well. Channah's room bloomed with the baby's layettes.

Money started to become an issue as soon as Channah moved in with Sophie and Max. Harris seemed to have no intention to support Channah or the baby. Channah never needed money for herself, but now for the baby, that was a different story.

No matter how much she sold her little embroidered monograms, it was still costly to buy thread and equipment needed for her handiwork. The different colors and crocheting equipment to make little caps and socks were expensive. Channah anticipated the baby would need a lot of clothes because babies grew so quickly.

Channah made clothes for Sophie's firstborn, Michael. Boys were different. It was okay for them to have more comfortable clothes, like overalls, to move around in. They had to be a little rough and ready.

When Channah felt the labor pains starting, she walked alone to Samaritan Hospital,[19] which was a number of blocks away from Sophie's house, another testament to Channah's strength.

The baby was born with a full head of fuzzy red hair. Channah was shocked at the baby's hair color. She had suspected the baby

---

[19] Samaritan Hospital was opened in 1892 by Russell Conwell in North Philadelphia. It is now known as Temple Hospital. Russell Conwell, when delivering his speech "Acres of Diamonds" thousands of times, founded Temple University. The university began as a night school for working men and women.

would be blond, just like the little Dutch boy she admired on Max's paint cans.

Channah named the baby Pessa Debrich.

# 26

## Raising the Redheaded Child

Harris, the absentee father, believed there was nothing special about his new redheaded daughter, except for her red hair, which was fantastic. Anyone who saw the baby instantly loved her. Channah never returned to Harris, and she brought up the little redhead by herself.

Channah's little Pessa Debrich later became Beatrice Deborah once she went to school.

In Harris's opinion, Channah had left him. So he didn't care if he had nothing to do with the new baby girl. Channah decided not to see Harris anymore. The baby was what Channah wanted.

The baby was all Channah could love. How could she love Harris? He was already in love with another woman. Channah's baby was the only one of Harris's children who had red hair.

Channah and Harris lived completely separate lives for the next thirty years. Channah never owned a home for just her and her daughter. Channah lived with Sophie for many years, except when Sophie moved to Texas.

Sophie's move left Channah looking for a place to live. She decided to move in to what was known as Molly's Madhouse. It was a boardinghouse where Temple University students would stay. Sophie sent Channah burlap sacks full of pecans. Channah would take Beatrice to the park with handfuls of pecans, which could've been their dinner. In Texas, one of Channah's relatives was known as the Pecan King. Pecan pies were probably not part of the menu as Channah was not known to be a good cook. The pecans would have been delicious in the *schnecken* that Sophie made.

Channah took Harris to court for him to provide money for Beatrice. Harris was eventually required by the Philadelphia court to provide child support. Harris countered that Channah was an unfit mother because she spoke little English.

Beatrice and Channah were both in court when the judge tested Beatrice's English. He asked her how she did in school. She replied that she received only the highest grades. "E. E. Nine," she answered.

The judge responded, "All you Jewish men are alike. You never want to pay child support." The judge granted Channah the money she needed.

How did Channah make money? She didn't sell her silver. Her needs were small, just clothes and food because her sister gave her a room.

Channah breastfed the baby until solid food was necessary. Beatrice ate whatever was available, as there was no baby food at this time. *Ic hut gekided fadir.* I chewed for you. This intimate act was what people did so babies could swallow their food, just like birds. No thought of germs or pollutants. Plenty of soups and stews were cooked to avoid chewing for the baby.

*Channah Spector, Helen's grandmother, with baby Beatrice.*

Harris's children knew his second wife, Channah, was their stepmother, but they could care less about their little red-haired half-sister who was born after Channah moved out. Their father, Harris, wanted to forget her existence and was not willing to help Channah raise his child.

# 27

## Beatrice

The little girl with the shockingly beautiful red hair was loved and spoiled by Channah and Sophie. Sophie, Max, and their (by then) five children returned from San Antonio, Texas when their general store was burned down by mobs of anti-Semites.

Beatrice's father, Harris, did not participate in her upbringing. He was focused on making money. He should have partnered with his brother, Amen. But Harris never believed that he could make money selling stationery. He was focused on scrap metal, which was in great demand in 1917 due to World War I.

For Amen, stationery would expand to office supplies, and many years later, office furniture. It was impossible to make a business completely in stationery and paper, or so Harris thought.

Beatrice grew up to be beautiful and loved hats of all shapes and sizes.

As a young girl, Beatrice tried to have a family connection with Harris's other children. However, the age difference was too great.

Beatrice as a student at
South Philadelphia High
School for Girls.

Amen Pomerantz, founder of
Pomerantz & Co. in Philadelphia,
at 1525 Chestnut Street. The
building boasts the first glass
curtain wall in the United States.

Her siblings thought of her only as a distant relative. Channah thought Beatrice should visit them. Harris would ask Beatrice sarcastically, "Is your mother still so tall?"

After Beatrice married Dr. Abraham Niemtzow, she had children of her own, first me, and three years later, Richard. They moved from Philadelphia to Freehold.

Beatrice's husband, Abraham, lost an older brother, Reuben, in 1917 to the influenza epidemic. Reuben had left home in Freehold and gone to New York City to work. I once saw a picture of Reuben in my grandfather Niemtzow's house on Vought Avenue in Freehold.

The house on Vought Avenue was a longtime residence of the Niemtzow family. Grandpop Niemtzow also had a property in the center of Freehold. This building had served as a military hospital during the Battle of Monmouth during the Revolutionary War. They would say that you could still see the bloodstains of the soldiers in the building. The battle took place in 1776, when the area was known as Monmouth, and was about fifty miles from Philadelphia.

Sometimes, Channah came to visit her ex-husband's children, Lillian, Esther, Frieda, Ernest, Minnie, and Francis, in Philadelphia. It was a nice visit for Beatrice to see her family and half-siblings.

Many years later, Harris's oldest daughter, Lillian, married a man named Mr. Duwell who was in the precious scrap metal business. He dealt with copper, platinum, brass, and bronze. Acquiring the metals involved a lot of traveling to seaports where the material was imported by ships and deposited at the docks and train yards. It was a different venture than Harris's steel scrap metal business.

I remember visiting *bubbe* at Sophie's house in Philadelphia. On one such visit, she gave me a little brown bag full of colored hair ribbons. Some of the ribbons were plaid and some were solid

*Beatrice Pomerantz,
the author's mother
(age twenty).*

colors. The assortment was my only memory of *bubbe's* gifts. She always had a certain way of expressing her emotions in colors. This was probably why her stained glass was so popular in Bremen. I loved the ribbons and, at times, I wondered if they demonstrated Channah's fondness for art and color. Perhaps she passed that passion to me, making me an architect and sometimes painter years later.

One day, Harris came for dinner in Freehold while Channah was visiting. I was just seven years old at the time. Harris came to see his daughter, Beatrice, and his grandchildren. During this visit, I noticed how large Channah's eyes were when she looked at Harris. The only explanation for her gaze was that Channah still loved Harris very much. "*Bubbe* what big eyes you have!" I exclaimed when I noticed it. The story of Little Red Riding Hood had come to my mind. In fact, I still have a Little Red Riding Hood doll sitting in my bedroom to this day.

*Three generations of women (Channah, Beatrice, and Helen).*

So much more would happen to this family than Channah had ever dreamed possible. If only Channah could have kept living. She made it to seventy-five years old and was active until the end.

However, before she died, she saw Harris again. Surprisingly, he came to visit his family in Freehold for a second time. I watched every movement my grandmother made. I knew that she still loved Grandpa Harris. He was important to her. I knew she would have been in favor of them getting back together. Beatrice did her best to fix up Channah's appearance. She put Channah's hair into large rolls. Her hair, which was now gray, was swept back from her face and she looked sophisticated. She used a device that sat on her head and secured the hair into a roll around her head. Channah's eyes were her most noticeable feature. They were large, grey, and happy. I didn't let this go unnoticed.

*Helen in 1958.*

## PART TWO

# Helen

In the seventeen years following Harris's last visit, I graduated from Freehold Regional High School and went on to graduate from Bryn Mawr College, where I majored in classical and Near Eastern archaeology. Accepted into University of Pennsylvania's Graduate School of Architecture, I was following the suggestion of my beloved archaeology professor Machteld Mellink that I channel my love for buildings of the past to buildings of the future.

# 28

## 1960, First Day of Architecture School

I wore a mint green shirtwaist dress that had a finely pleated skirt. My long dark hair was styled in a French twist. I had a narrow waist topped off with a voluptuous chest. I found my way to the original dental school building, a dull red brick building that was a product of the 1880s and took up about half a city block on campus. I entered my first class in Penn's Graduate Architecture School with excitement and big dreams. It was a required course about building structures and the rest of the class was already seated in the amphitheater. I was determined to become one of the greatest architects, so I briskly walked to the front row and took a seat.

As I walked down the steps, passing the rest of my classmates, I heard a young man comment, "This is too much too early in the morning." Straight out of Bryn Mawr College, an all-girls school

*Helen at her drafting table at the University of Pennsylvania, School of Architecture in 1962.*

at the time, I found myself to be the only woman in a class of forty-two men. I took my seat at the front, ignoring the comment.

I would later discover that I was the first woman to attend the new graduate school of architecture started by Dean G. Holmes Perkins. Under Perkins's leadership, I hoped that I would get a fair shake among the men. I never wanted any special treatment because I was a woman. The only thing I wanted was to be seen as equal to my classmates. I knew I could keep up with the male students in my class. On this first day, I was most anxious to start my architecture training.

It would be an exciting first year for me. Learning to navigate through a new graduate program recommended to me by a friend, Charles William III, I strived to be the best architect in my class. As with any school experience, I made some friends, but I was mostly engrossed in my schoolwork.

Perkins set up the architecture school, but Louis I. Kahn ran the master's program. The rest of the faculty was installed by Perkins, and they were illustrious and wonderful men. My professors at the school were Robert Geddes, Tim Vreeland, and Romaldo Giurgola, who later became the dean of the architecture school at Columbia University. Additionally, Kahn was the leading architect in the world while he taught the master's program.

On the very first day of school, we were brought outdoors on the university's campus to observe everything, which they later tested us on. Perkins had organized the curriculum to no longer emphasize the Beaux-Arts school traditions of Paris. Later, I worked with Norman Rice, who had been a Beaux-Arts man. He was a teaching partner for Kahn. I remember at one point he had stood over me, looking at my drawings, and said, "Don't etch that. Etchers, beware!" He was telling me to work faster.

We were taught to design quickly, in ten days or less. We designed churches, houses, ski huts, and more. When I designed a town house, I was told that my design was something the jury had wanted to live in.

The summer after I graduated from Bryn Mawr, before coming to the University of Pennsylvania, I worked for the architect Noboru Kobayashi as a draftsperson in Red Bank, New Jersey. I had lied and said that I was already attending the architecture school at Penn under the direction of Kahn, who at the time wouldn't have known me from Abraham Lincoln.

To get to Kobayashi's office, I had to borrow my brother's red convertible and would drive by cornfields and Black Angus cattle roaming in green pastures. One morning, I was driving so fast that I was stopped by a police officer for speeding. I received a ticket.

*Helen and fellow students, Dick Nordhaus and Sydney Guberman, at the University of Pennsylvania, School of Architecture (1962).*

When I returned home after work and told my parents and brother about the ticket, it didn't go over well. I always wondered why my brother was given a car and I was not. When I had to borrow my parents' car, it seemed like they waited in the driveway for me to return it.

The summer went by and I designed a couple of different offices for my employer. Although I did not have any prior experience, I had managed to get hired. I wondered if it was due to my figure and beautiful long hair.

When I did finally start the graduate program at Penn, I moved into the graduate residences located at 34th and Walnut Streets. I had a roommate for the first time in my life. I remember that she had a terrible case of acne and after just two weeks, she decided to leave school. I was left to live on my own. Still, I wasn't satisfied with the dorm and asked my parents to find me an apartment.

Surprisingly, they agreed. I was a free agent. There were no curfews and I had all the freedom I could ever imagine. My father went berserk. He didn't want me loose in Philadelphia.

I had a great wardrobe and a long dark ponytail. My mother and I bought furniture for my apartment, including a classic mid-century modern two-piece hand-blown glass vase with an unusual blue glass orb that probably didn't originally come with the vase. We rented a truck with a driver and filled it with my belongings and new purchases for my apartment. My father watched from his dental office, which was in our residence, as the truck left my childhood home on its way to Philadelphia.

It empowered me to know that I was the only woman in a class of forty-two men. After Bryn Mawr's academic and social restrictions, I felt free and inspired. I was thankful that Perkins had accepted and approved my credentials. Prior to my acceptance at the school, he asked me for drawing samples. When I came to his office, I showed him my drawings of nude women. I was unsure of how he would respond. But, to my surprise, my chutzpah and drawings got me accepted into the university.

As a full-fledged Penn architecture student, I suffered through as well as enjoyed my coursework. I became more proficient at designing and I was being trained to produce architecture at a fast pace with serious appropriate designs. I was trained by the *charrettes*, which would pop up when you least expected them. I also had overnight design problems. It was a rigorous program that kept all of us students on our toes.

I focused a lot of energy on creating good renderings for my designs. One professor helped me out with perfecting my renderings. He even taught a class in which I was his only student. I drew in ink using an alternator and rapidograph. I also learned how to draw trees in plan, as architects drew them, perspectives and thirty-degree isometrics. Eventually, I learned how to execute terrific perspectives. However, I was never satisfied with my perspectives and depended mostly on sections and plans to express my buildings.

My first experience with sexism in the classroom occurred when I was forced to take a predesign course while the rest of the class took a more advanced entry-level design course. As a result, it took me an extra year to graduate. The upside to taking this course was that it was taught by the Polish female architect Siasia Nowicki, who was magnificent. I became her number-one student. She taught me skills that I never would have learned elsewhere. After a while, I started to dress like her.

This was also fortuitous because I met my future husband, Mickey, during my second year in the design class. This was the design class that I thought I was supposed to take the year before. I was also a year ahead of the rest of my class in structural engineering. So in my last year, I only had to focus on my student thesis and take just one advanced engineering course.

Next to Nowicki's office was a workshop with a band saw, jigsaw, and vise used to make architectural models. I found out that I loved to make models out of chipboard, basswood, and cork. The whole top floor of the architecture school building was a design studio partitioned for students with their own drafting tables and equipment. Many student football games were held here too, thanks to the high ceilings. Players were able to put a spin on the ball and arc it high enough for it to come down to the receiver. Due to large windows, there was a tremendous amount of light in the space, which illuminated our work areas.

There was a mezzanine level, which had the coffee machine, where we would gather and enjoy hot cups of coffee. It also served as an entrance to the architectural library, which contained all of the relevant catalogs and books that were needed to complete the program successfully. I spent a lot of time in the library. I would peruse the card catalogs and journals, such as *Architectural Record* and *Aujourd'hui*, for inspiration and was always impressed by the library's offerings.

The building was situated across from Franklin Field, and I would often hear the cheering crowds during a Saturday football game in the autumn. The relaxed atmosphere of Saturday classes enabled me to browse the other studios for other courses that were taught, such as sculpture, painting, and other art classes.

Perkins wanted a mixture of artistic disciplines offered in the building so we were exposed to different concepts and ideas, somewhat like the Beaux-Arts school in Paris. They mixed several disciplines together with the architects' works.

# 29

## Meeting Mickey

The first day of my second year in architectural school, I met Roger "Mickey" Sherman Pratt. He sat behind me in one of my design classes. When I first saw him, I couldn't take my eyes off of him. He was such a good-looking guy, with very attractive blue eyes and blond hair. It's a good thing I was the only woman in the class or else all of the girls would have challenged me for him. Whenever I saw him outside of class, he was smoking a pipe and wearing a tweed jacket.

Our relationship began in February 1962, once Mickey convinced me to go out with him. Mickey had claimed to be half Jewish, which wasn't a complete lie since his stepfather, Joseph Lash, was Jewish. I invited Mickey over to my apartment for dinner. I bought some steaks to cook and Mickey supplied the ice cream for dessert.

We got along fantastically. I never thought I could feel so excited about being in someone's presence. He told me all about

*Roger Sherman Pratt (Mickey), about 1957.*

*Bathing beauty photo of Helen in 1960.*

*Helen Niemtzow, about 1962.*

*Roger Sherman Pratt, about 1962.*

his family, the powerful Pratt family of Glen Cove, New York City, and Connecticut. He shared how he even spent a summer in the White House as a child, with his mother's good friend, Eleanor Roosevelt. I was drawn in by his stories and exotic life.

It was just ten days after that first dinner that Mickey suggested that we get married. What was an exciting and whirlwind romance turned into something unbelievably invigorating. He bought me a diamond ring with a stone much too big for a girl in her twenties from my uncle's jewelry store in Philadelphia.

From that moment forward, I went on to meet the Pratt family, including Mickey's German mother, Trude Lash, and his step-father, Joe Lash. To my surprise, my soon-to-be new family had very unique connections, one of them being Eleanor Roosevelt.

# 30

## Learning About the Pratt Empire

My entrance into this new world which included U.S. presidents, first ladies, and oil fortunes came through my marriage to Mickey (nicknamed that as a child because of his big ears). The Pratt family, while of high social status, also had a complicated legacy through its association with John D. Rockefeller's Standard Oil empire.

The Pratt family patriarch, Charles Pratt, was a pioneer in the U.S. petroleum industry, establishing Astral Oil Works, a kerosene refinery in Brooklyn, New York, in the mid-nineteenth century. Through clever marketing, Astral Oil's high-quality kerosene became common in households around the world. In 1874, Rockefeller purchased Astral Oil for an undisclosed price. The acquisition made Pratt a very wealthy man and a partner in Rockefeller's Standard Oil Trust.

In World War II, Rockefeller's Standard Oil played a dark role, supplying both the U.S. and the Nazis with fuel. For this, it was

*Charles Pratt, Roger's great-grandfather.*

fined a mere $5,000 by the U.S. government after it was discovered it was supplying the enemy.[20] However, this punishment did not quite fit the crime because the U.S. was dependent on Standard Oil as well. It was just a slap on the wrist. Philadelphia manufacturers[21] were similarly accused of supplying the Nazis with vitally indispensable war supplies. Without this help, Nazi war progress would have slowed, and they would have had to look elsewhere for assistance.

---

[20] Charles Higham, Trading with the Enemy: An Expose of the Nazi-American Money-Plot 1933–1949 (New York: Delacorte Press, 1983).

[21] Swedish company SKF had a large factory in Philadelphia that produced ball bearings, which are used in virtually every mechanical tool including tanks, planes, trucks, and other military equipment.

# 31

## The Relatives of Roger Sherman Pratt

I decided finally to write about the special dinner that I had in 1962 with the former first lady of the United States, Eleanor Roosevelt. The dinner was an overture to my wedding to Mickey.

On May 26, 1962, I married Mickey in a rabbi's study in Manhattan. This was promptly followed by a dinner with just our immediate family members.

Mickey was the son of a wealthy American, Eliot Deming Pratt, and a German woman, Gertrude "Trude" Wenzel Pratt. Trude left Germany with her new American husband, Eliot Pratt, a fellow student at Freiburg University, in the early 1930s, around the time that the Nazis took over. Before Trude left Germany, she was a journalist for an overtly anti-Nazi newspaper. Soon after she departed, her office was searched, ransacked, and the newspaper was shut down.

*Trude Wenzel Lash.*

Prior to Trude's career in journalism, she studied at the University of Heidelberg. She received a PhD in philosophy in 1930 from the University of Freiburg, where she had met Eliot, a grandson of Charles Pratt.

During her years of study at the University of Freiburg, Trude traveled to the U.S., where she taught at Hunter College while completing research at Columbia University. Trude's student years were ambitious and she was known as an intellectual.

During her time in the U.S. as an exchange student, Trude became heavily involved in the International Student Service (ISS), a group established and led by Joseph Lash, who would later become her second husband. When she moved with Eliot to the U.S., she tried to help refugees escape the Nazis through the ISS.

Trude had a brother, Heinz Wenzel, who was seldom mentioned. He served in the German army during World War

*Aerial view of the Killenworth Estate in Glen Cove, Long Island, built by Roger's grandfather, George Pratt.*

II. While Trude became embedded in the American side of the conflict, her brother was her political opposite.

Trude and Eliot were married in Baden-Württemberg in 1932. They immediately left for the U.S., where they would take up residence at the Pratt's Killenworth Estate in Glen Cove, New York. Eliot's father, George DuPont Pratt, built the enormous estate on Long Island's Gold Coast on property his father, Charles Pratt, had acquired in 1890.

Trude was fascinated by Killenworth and the large number of gardeners that were required to take care of its grounds. She once told me that the entire estate employed sixty-five gardeners.

Killenworth was sold to the Soviet Union in 1951 and now serves as a Russian weekend retreat. In the early 1980s, Glen Cove residents accused the Russians of using Killenworth for espionage. In response to the accusations, the city of Glen Cove revoked the Russians' beach privileges.[22]

In 2016, in one of his final acts as president, Barack Obama expelled many Russian diplomats and seized some of the American estates they occupied. However, Killenworth still remains in Russia's possession.

Trude and Eliot had three children together: Peter, Vera, and Roger, whom I would marry. Trude and Eliot divorced during the summer of 1943. Shortly after her divorce from Eliot was finalized, Trude married Joe Lash, making him Mickey's stepfather.

---

[22] John McQuiston, "Russians Long a Thorny Issue," *New York Times*, Aug. 8, 1982

# 32

## The Meeting of Eleanor Roosevelt, Joseph Lash, and Trude Wenzel Lash

Decades before my marriage, Eleanor formally met Lash at the House Un-American Activities Committee (HUAC), also called the Dies Committee of Un-American Affairs of the House of Representatives. The committee was considered a communist witch hunt operation.[23] At the time, FDR was president and Eleanor was America's first lady. It was at these committee meetings, when Lash was questioned about his involvement with the American Youth Congress and the infiltration of communism, that Lash and Eleanor's relationship truly started. According to

---

[23] Created in 1938 to investigate those suspected of having communist ties.

*Joseph Lash and Eleanor Roosevelt in 1939.*

Lash, in one of his pieces on Eleanor, they first met on a train to Washington, D.C.

After a meeting of the Dies Committee, Eleanor invited Lash and his codefendants to dinner at the White House. The dinner was the start of a friendship between Eleanor and Lash that would last her lifetime. However, Eleanor's involvement with the Lash family, both with Joseph and Trude, appeared to be more complicated than history has fully recorded.

It was a few years after Lash and Eleanor's initial meeting that President Roosevelt heard from the FBI of an alleged intimate relationship between them. FDR reportedly imploded and within ten hours, shipped Lash, a sergeant in the U.S. Air Force, from his station in the U.S. to the war zone of Guadalcanal in the Solomon Islands. Guadalcanal is located northeast off the Australian coast.

*Joseph Lash.*

While an intimate relationship between Joe and Eleanor was never confirmed, the FBI still reported one to President Roosevelt. It allegedly took place in 1943 at the Blackstone Hotel in Chicago. Despite the fifteen-year age difference between Eleanor and Lash, FDR's drastic move of sending Lash to the Pacific Theater during the height of World War II certainly raises questions. During Lash's assignment at Guadalcanal as a weatherman, Eleanor scheduled a trip there as a representative of the Red Cross. She inspected Red Cross installations, visiting the Christmas Islands, Bora Bora, Samoa, Fiji, New Zealand, Australia, and Guadalcanal.[24]

In Eleanor's letters to Lash immediately following their time together in Guadalcanal, she said, "How I hated to have you leave last night. When the war is over, I hope I never have to be long

---

[24] A full list of her stops includes: Christmas Islands; Penrhyn Island; Bora Bora, Society Islands; Aitutaki, Cook Islands; Tutuila; Samoa; Fiji; Auckland, New Zealand; Wellington, New Zealand; Rotorua, New Zealand; Sydney, Australia; Canberra, Australia; Melbourne, Australia; Rockhampton, Australia; Cairns, Australia; Brisbane, Australia; Nouméa, New Caledonia; Espiritu Santo, Guadalcanal; and Wallis.

away from you. It was so wonderful to be with you; the whole trip now seems to me to be worthwhile."[25] It was a brash move for Eleanor to follow Lash to the most dangerous war zone, and then to seemingly admit, albeit in private letters, that Joe was a large reason she made the trip.

At the time, her tour of the Pacific Theater was no easy feat. It was still the height of World War II. In fact, Guadalcanal was bombed the night before Eleanor arrived and the night after she left.

The Japanese took Burma, Indonesia, the Philippines, and attempted to take Midway Island. However, the U.S. developed radar and Midway was a short, decisive naval battle that lasted less than a week. The U.S. transitioned from defensive to offensive as a result of Guadalcanal. The threat of a Japanese invasion was eliminated as a result of these two battles. The battle was almost entirely fought in aircraft. During the battle of Midway, the U.S. lost 292 aircraft, four carriers, and suffered twenty-five hundred casualties.

Putting his and Eleanor's close friendship aside, shortly after he returned to the States, Joe married Trude on November 10, 1944, at Eleanor's private cottage, Val-Kill, on the Roosevelt's estate in Hyde Park, New York. Whether this marriage was arranged to distract from the alleged affair between Eleanor and Joe is not certain. However, it was not long after Trude's divorce from Eliot Pratt that Eleanor introduced Trude to Joe. Eleanor and Trude were not only to remain the closest of friends, but Trude's three children spent the summer of 1944 at the White House, and Mickey became very close to Eleanor at the time.

---

[25] Blanche Wiesen Cook, *Eleanor Roosevelt, Volume 3: The War Years and After, 1939–1962* (New York: Viking, 2016).

Trude was wealthy from her divorce from Eliot and had become a political activist in New York. Trude first met Eleanor at Democratic political parties in 1943. Trude's friendship with Eleanor was so close that the Soviets wanted to use Trude to elicit information on Eleanor and the White House—even though the Soviet Union and the U.S. were presumably allies during World War II.

The close friendship between Eleanor and Joe seems to have persisted in both letter writing and events, and it benefitted Trude. In a way, Trude was a double agent with two roles to play: one as the wife of Joe Lash, who had communist sympathies, and the other as a close friend of Eleanor. It appears that Eleanor, Trude, and Joe were closely intertwined.

# 33

## The Venona Decryption

A Venona decryption[26] from May 1943 disclosed that the Soviets were considering recruiting Trude for Soviet intelligence. The decryption proposed using Trude to process information from Eleanor Roosevelt.[27] It also suggested bringing Elizabeth Zarubina, who handled many high-level important cases, into close touch with Trude.[28]

It is difficult to tell from the sparse and partially declassified files the extent of the relationship between the Soviets and Trude, or if such a relationship ever existed. The possibility of such a conspiracy would cast a new shadow on the friendship between Eleanor and Trude.

---

[26] Liza Mundy, "Code Name: Venona," *Smithsonian*, September 2018. 30–39.
[27] See decrypted Venona transmission from New York to Moscow mentioning Trude Wenzel Pratt Lash. The transmission was sent on May 26, 1943.
[28] Venona transmission, New York to Moscow, May 26, 1943, 786–787.

*PRIVATE*

95

USSR ⬛⬛⬛⬛

Ref. No: ⬛⬛⬛ (of 15/10/1956)

Issued: ⬛/22/5/1962

Copy No: *204*

RE-ISSUE

MENTION OF "PROCESSING" OF "CAPTAIN's" WIFE (1943)

From: NEW YORK

To: MOSCOW

Nos: 786-787                        26 May <u>43</u>

[Part I]                 [Two-part message complete]

    To VIKTOR.[i]

       For processing[OXORXLENIX] "CAPTAIN's[KAPITAN]"[ii] wife we [2 groups unrecovered] her great friend Gertrude PRATT, wife of the well-known Wealthy Elliot PRATT

[15 groups unrecovered]

patroness and guide. In this line contact is being maintained with her by Aleksej [C;SOK]IRKIN[iii], the official representative of the MOSCOW Anti-Fascist Student Committee [X who arrived] [6 groups unrecovered] "Syndicate". [iv] PRATT [Dx displays] great interest in life in the USSR and Soviet

[38 groups unrecovered]

the latter circumstance for bringing "VARDO"[v] into close touch with her with a view to

[119 groups unrecovered or unrecoverable]

or scientific worker.

<u>Distribution</u>                                   [Continued overleaf]

⬛⬛⬛⬛⬛⬛⬛⬛⬛

⬛⬛⬛⬛

*The Venona Decryption, 1943.*

Trude and Joe Lash lived on 11th Street in the Greenwich Village area of New York City in a house where they raised Trude's children, and a son, Jonathan Lash, born in 1945. In 1950, Joe Lash got a job at the *New York Post* covering the United Nations. In 1952, at which time Eleanor was an ambassador to the United Nations, Joe edited two books of FDR's letters with Elliot Roosevelt. In 1961, Lash published his first biography. It was about former UN Secretary-General Dag Hammarskjöld.

Lash went on to publish several books on the Roosevelts, particularly on Eleanor. In 1971, he published *Eleanor and Franklin,* for which he won the Pulitzer Prize for Biography. In addition, Joe won the National Book Award in biography and the Francis Parkman Prize of the Society of American Historians. I attended the celebration for Joe's Pulitzer at the 21 Club in New York City and even helped to organize the dinner.

Trude went on to work for the Human Rights Commission at the UN before moving to the Citizens Commission for Children in New York City.

My own experience with the matter of Eleanor, Trude, and Joe doesn't add much more information. However, it sheds light on the importance and everlasting effects of the Joe Lash and Eleanor Roosevelt relationship. Their friendship lasted until her death in 1962, and I can only imagine the friction it may have caused in such a high-profile marriage as the one between a U.S. president and first lady.

When Mickey and I were getting ready to marry, I was in Trude and Joe's house sleeping on the couch in Joe's study. I awoke one morning with Mickey and Trude staring down at me. They had been trying to wake me up. I overheard Mickey say to Trude, "Look at her while she sleeps; she looks so beautiful." Mickey was so proud to show me off to his mother.

It might have been this day that I overheard part of a conversation between Elaine Egee, Peter Pratt's wife, and Trude. They were talking about Guadalcanal and Joe's expulsion to the island by FDR. There was a hush and the conversation stopped as I entered the room. Still, so many years later, Guadalcanal was a sensitive subject.

# 34

## My Future In-Laws

Joe Lash was treated like a king in his home. Trude protected Joe and had us all remain quiet while Joe wrote his editorials for the *New York Post.* The writing took place after he discussed the pieces with Dorothy Schiff, the paper's owner and publisher. It was hard for us to keep the house quiet while Joe worked because Trude's grandchildren from Peter and Elaine Pratt lived in an apartment on the ground floor. I wondered if one day I would have to share a house with Trude and Joe. I hoped not.

Eleanor never came to see Trude and Joe while I was there, though we had many dinners and cocktail parties that would have been appropriate for Eleanor to attend. Eleanor had a very busy life and I never got the impression that Eleanor and Joe had any romantic feelings between them. I also noticed that Trude never acted suspiciously of Joe.

A sexual relationship in the past between Joe and Eleanor was hard to believe or imagine, especially since Eleanor was fifteen years older than Joe and married to one of the most respected presidents in U.S. history. Other than hearing Trude comment to Elaine about Guadalcanal, I never would have suspected anything.

I rarely got upset or felt out of touch with Trude and Joe. But one incident bothered me greatly when we were discussing the wedding reception. Trude said that the party, which was planned for Manhattan's Cosmopolitan Club, would break my father financially. I never knew how much the reception cost, but it had to be expensive because both dinner and hors d'oeuvres were served. Trude wasn't looking out for his financial well-being. Instead, she was trying to act as if he couldn't afford it and not offering to help. I took it as a slight and later told Mickey that maybe we should call the wedding off.

# 35

## Arrival for Dinner

A few weeks prior to mine and Mickey's wedding, Eleanor invited us to her apartment for a private dinner. I didn't think it at the time, but I suspect Trude must have scheduled this dinner to get Eleanor's approval of my marriage to Mickey. If Eleanor liked me, it would take place as planned. Mickey and I couldn't refuse an invitation to dinner with Mrs. Roosevelt.

"It will just be the three of you," Trude told me again and again, impressing upon me the significance of the event.

I really hoped everything would go well at the dinner. At the time, I did not realize just how special the opportunity was. I had seen many pictures of Eleanor, but it would be my first meeting with her in person.

I had nothing to do with the arrangement. I was simply given the address of Eleanor's apartment on East 74th Street in New York. It was not far from Mickey's father's place on East 71st Street, but it was a world away from Freehold.

*Eleanor Roosevelt in 1962.*

Eleanor's dinner took place a week before our wedding. All seemed to be planned for us. Why didn't I question anything? I didn't even question what to wear. My clothes were never a problem. I always had plenty of outfits, both old and new. My father just kept paying for the things I bought for the wedding. I enjoyed getting most of my trousseau from the exclusive Nan Duskin shop in Philadelphia.

I also shopped at Esther Pomerantz, my aunt's shop on 17th Street in Philadelphia, for my mother's outfits for the wedding and the reception. They were two quite fashionable blue linen dresses.

At Bryn Mawr, my sole responsibility was to distinguish myself academically and then become a fine architect in Penn's graduate architecture program. I did not get sidetracked by clothes, but I loved dressing well while in school.

Whatever I wore to any occasion was appropriate, tasteful, and beautiful under my mother's watchful eye. Mom and I loved to be stylish and we shopped well together. For this occasion, we used our best taste. While I can't remember all the specifics of my outfit, I do remember settling on a fitted pink Pucci dress to wear to Eleanor's dinner.

If I had gone shopping by myself, which a young woman of twenty-three should do, I may not have bought such an appropriate dress. I don't remember everything I looked at, but all of the dresses looked good on me. This I knew. My mother was creative at decorating the two of us. I also knew Mickey thought I was especially beautiful and intelligent, which helped my confidence a great deal.

Mickey and I were embarking on what any other young couple wanted, a happy and loving marriage. But before that could

*Eleanor Roosevelt holding the Universal Declaration of Human Rights in 1949.*

happen, we would have dinner with Eleanor Roosevelt, the former U.S. first lady and former U.S. ambassador to the United Nations. This dinner would be with the person whom some believe to be the greatest woman in modern U.S. history.

# 36

## *Eleanor's Apartment*

Mickey and I were standing outside the front door of Eleanor's building around 5 p.m., both of us sufficiently spruced up.

Following FDR's death, Eleanor had gone on to establish her own place in world history. More than a decade before our cozy meeting, Eleanor had been involved in "The Universal Declaration of Human Rights," which she co-wrote with the Drafting Committee[29] of the United Nations Commission on Human Rights. It stands out as one of the most important documents ever created.[30]

Did I know all this when I climbed the stairs to Eleanor's home on 74th Street in New York City that evening in 1962? Probably

---

[29] Eleanor was the chair of the Drafting Committee. Other well-known members include John Peters Humphrey, René Cassin, Charles Malik, P. C. Chang, and Hansa Mehta.

[30] Adopted on December 10, 1948, with forty-eight countries in favor and eight abstaining, the document is not a binding treaty, but it is the foundation for several other UN human rights agreements and a positive outgrowth of World War II.

*Eleanor's home at 55 East 74th Street in New York City.*

not. I was so excited to meet Eleanor that I even ignored the Greek-inspired columns framing the front entrance to her house.

I would later discover that these columns were Ionic. I don't remember who let us in. I just know that I walked through a doorway whose doorjambs were decorated with classical details. The entrance felt like the Propylaea, the ancient gateway to the Acropolis in Athens, Greece. How could I, an architecture student, have overlooked this significant decoration?

These wonderful details would be useful someday to understand who designed the building, and I marveled at who could have chosen them for a twentieth century entrance. I would have liked to live there and wallow in its classical beauty. According to my professor, Nowicki, an entrance should "whistle at you," and I found this to be entirely true in the case of Eleanor's house.

# 37

## Talking with Eleanor

I was anxious to tell Mrs. Roosevelt who I was, and I was so sure that I was the perfect bride for Roger Sherman Pratt—an heir, no less, to a part of the Standard Oil fortune. I knew that this dinner was a test of sorts for Eleanor's approval of my marriage to Mickey, something that Trude clearly wanted. I'll never know if my being Jewish fit in somewhere in this "interview." I did not imagine that the dinner was conceived to tighten the bond between Trude and Eleanor, me and Trude, or both.

I was going to be entertained by America's beloved Eleanor Roosevelt. Yet I had little appreciation for the magnitude of the occasion. I had worked hard all my life for a moment like this, but only much later did I understand its enormity. I knew that Eleanor, though she did not run our country, surely had a huge role as ambassador to the UN and was a champion of human rights.

I took the dinner invitation in stride. It was my reward for working hard and being raised well. I did not stop to question the

*Trude and Joe Lash with Eleanor Roosevelt in the 1940s.*

purpose of the dinner and simply went along with it. I didn't think it was anything to be agitated about. At the time, I did not understand the implications of this marriage and the dinner invitation.

I only fully remember, some fifty years later, that this was indeed an interview. I needed Eleanor's stamp of approval, the ultimate acceptance, for the wedding to proceed to the son of Eleanor's very close friends, Trude and Joe Lash. I would become aware of the degree of Joe's closeness only after reading his books about Eleanor years later.

I was not prepared for the woman who greeted me at the top of the stairs at 55 East 74th Street. This was the second floor of the building that Eleanor called home. She co-owned the home with David and Edna Gurewitsch.[31] The building was no White House,

---

[31] David Gurewitsch was Eleanor's physician. He accompanied her on her trip to Europe. He and his wife, Edna, were very close friends of the Roosevelts.

but still the house of America's former first lady, Anna Eleanor Roosevelt. Looking at her, starting from her feet up, she had on ghillie tie shoes, a casual outfit, and a necklace of pearls around her neck. Her hair was pulled back and lifted off her neck.

On the steps to the second floor, this woman of seventy-eight years appeared even taller than her stately six feet. Her welcoming smile lit up the stairs. Later, I learned we could have taken an elevator. But when you're in your early twenties, an elevator is hardly necessary. The stairs led into a large living room with high ceilings and a large semicircular bay window. I remember a big table with all sorts of bric-a-brac on it in front of the window. I was sitting face-to-face with Eleanor.

Eleanor had lovely skin, simply unblemished. It looked so soft. In general, she was not as unattractive as reputed. Her teeth did not appear to protrude. She was about the same height as my grandmother Channah, who stood about five feet and ten inches. This height is also the same as Trude's. I was five inches shorter and had to stand on my toes to talk to either woman.

Eleanor was high waisted. What I remember most was her face, which was pleasant, and her hairstyle revealed a very high forehead. She had excellent posture and sat up straight. Her clothing was muted neutral colors and may have been beige, a beige jacket over a beige skirt with some kind of dark shirt. She wasn't fashion oriented—nothing like my mother whose figure and wardrobe were always *au courant*.

What I remember most are her shoes. They were practical with low heels and laces. The shoes were more memorable than the rest of her outfit, which seemed to cover her figure for warmth rather than decoration. She presented herself with an air of correctness.

Certainly, the windows seemed translucent with only white lace curtains letting in the light, which penetrated the room. Eleanor

*Trude Lash standing next to Eleanor (1955).*

was doing well; she was smiling when she had led us into the room. She hadn't offered Mickey a seat, but he looked very comfortable wandering around. He gave me the impression that he had been there before. I never asked. Now, as I recall the initial welcome, it is quite clear that I was about to be interviewed, measured for my worthiness. I was being tested by Eleanor. She appeared to take her assignment as judge for Trude Lash very seriously.

Trude was checking me out through Eleanor. I jumped right in and played the game. I avoided my recollection of being called a "dirty Jew" by forgetting the ridiculous label altogether. What is a dirty Jew? With such a label, I had managed to become a student at the University of Pennsylvania Graduate School of Architecture, where I was the only woman in the class.

In the living room, as Mrs. Roosevelt sat on her upholstered couch, 1 knew 1 could count on my intelligence to guide me. To calm my nerves, 1 imagined that Eleanor was just an ordinary old lady. So what if she had been the wife of one of our greatest and most beloved presidents.

# 38

## The Interview

"Tell me about yourself," Eleanor said.

"This is easy enough," I thought.

Starting to get hungry, I wondered if I could confide in her that I would eat two hoagies for lunch every day with ham, cheese, mustard, and mayonnaise at Penn from Frank's food truck. I ate so much, hoping it would make me as strong as the men in my class.

I thought better than to share this information and started to talk of my goals. These were from my heart, and I believed that Mickey could be a happy partner in achieving these goals.

Looking at Eleanor sitting across from me, I said, "Mickey is my classmate and only a month younger than me."

I went on to say that being architects seems like the perfect career for both of us, me especially. I told Mrs. Roosevelt about my devotion to my schoolwork. I said that, more than anything, I wanted to be an archaeologist and being an architect would bring me closer to this objective. I told her that architects are needed to evaluate the ruins uncovered by archaeologists. The evidence from buildings and other objects destroyed by time speaks of civilizations and people that have since disappeared.

I told Mrs. Roosevelt that I loved being an archaeologist and that Professor Mellink at Bryn Mawr College had pointed me in the direction of architecture and said being an archaeological architect would make me invaluable professionally. I would always have employment. There are very few acknowledged archaeological architects in the world.

I didn't tell Eleanor about a phone discussion with my mother when she questioned me as I discussed my future career as an archaeologist. An archaeologist was not enough, my mother had said, "You need to belong to a traditional profession." Being an architect was satisfactory to her.

What Mrs. Roosevelt saw before her was an excited young woman about to marry a fellow architecture student. This young woman did not comprehend the potential of this astounding interview or the potential of this incredible marriage to an heir of Standard Oil.

I didn't grasp the situation in its entirety. Even if I knew then what I know now, would it have made a difference? Would I still be marrying Mickey and having dinner with Mrs. Roosevelt? Would my goals have changed if I knew the full scope of this marriage, which could adversely affect my intention to be an archaeological architect?

Mrs. Roosevelt was pleasant to me during our dinner. It did not enter my mind that Trude had asked her friend, Eleanor, to evaluate her future daughter-in-law to see if I was right for Mickey and how I would fit in with the rest of the family. I suddenly was given what one would call the third degree. The questions, rather clear, were not preplanned, or did not appear to be. Had they not trusted Mickey's judgment?

In my interview, I thought Eleanor was just curious about a young architecture student who was somewhere in her early twenties. On the contrary, did she wonder whether I was a fortune hunter or a social climber? The simple answer was that I wanted only to show that I met the standards of my great-grandfather, Rabbi Slotskov, the grand rabbi of Vilna, Lithuania during the mid-nineteenth century, which was the intellectual epicenter of Jewish scholarship at the time.

How could I portray this to Eleanor? Had she ever met someone like my great-grandfather? He was the most intellectual relative in my family's history, far superior to anyone Mickey could offer. My aim was to make him proud of me. I hoped to do this as an archaeological architect.

Here I was studying to be in a profession usually reserved for men. Did Eleanor know this? Did she know what a competitive profession architecture is? Especially for a woman, to tackle such a field is very challenging.

I knew that Mickey was no cheat when he asked me for copies of exams I had taken previously. I thought little of his request at the time, but realized that I had worked much harder to prepare for exams than he did. I gave them to him and felt guilty immediately, but I wanted him to succeed.

This honest thinking was intruded upon when Mrs. Roosevelt asked me what had convinced me to study architecture. Easy question. The answer went back to Bryn Mawr and Professor Mellink.

Professor Mellink wrote recommendations for me to attend graduate architecture school at the University of Pennsylvania and Harvard University. I was accepted to both. On the advice of Charles William III, a friend of Arthur Steinburg, both graduate students at Penn and taking courses in archaeology at Bryn Mawr,

I chose Penn, the school where Louis I. Kahn[32] was teaching and lecturing. I am so glad I did.

Why did I feel so comfortable with Mrs. Roosevelt? Was it because she seemed to like me? I knew I was prepared for anything she would say. I noticed she stayed away from all subjects that would be difficult for us to discuss, such as religion, news, and my parents. The fact that I wanted to be an archaeological architect seemed to have escaped her. I guess that it was a strange goal.

Whatever she asked me, I had an answer ready. I would say I had a firm goal to become an archaeological architect. I would be a "rare bird," a unique product of Bryn Mawr College, where Professor Mellink herself prompted me to be one of the few archaeological architects in the world.

---

[32] Louis I. Kahn is a famous twentieth century architect. He taught at University of Pennsylvania in Philadelphia and built Richard's Medical Center, the design of which separated mechanical equipment from the rest of the building.

# 39

## *Dinner with Eleanor*

None of my other classmates in architecture school, a highly competitive group, pursued me romantically. They were not willing to subject themselves to Mickey's wrath and possessiveness. They did not want to challenge me as a person while also challenging me as a fellow architecture student. Mickey thought I was a prize and he was amazed that he had won the contest for my hand. However, I did not like his architecture designs. I never told him. I just strived to make my designs the best: simple and clean.

I thought everything was going well, even though the interview with Eleanor dragged on. I grew hungrier and was ready to eat whatever smelled so good. A little old lady stepped into the room and announced, "Dinner is ready," just in time. Mrs. Roosevelt's housekeeper wore a white apron over a simple, dark uniform with her hair pulled into a tight roll. She was also very quiet and not intrusive.

I didn't see him, but I was certain Mickey had found himself a drink. How did he become so comfortable in this situation? After I had familiarized myself with Eleanor's living room, the interrogation continued over a pot roast dinner.

We moved to the dining room and sat at a small, intimate bridge table adjacent to the main dining room table. It was just the three of us: Eleanor, Mickey, and me.

I did not care about china or silver patterns and can only assume we were using family utensils that had been passed down to Eleanor. The dishes were an ecru color edged with gold, which was the style of Lenox china, a popular brand for newly married couples. I was never particularly keen on this design. I preferred my blue-on-blue china by Spode that I chose after Mickey and I married. It never dawned on me that Eleanor, in 1962, could be using White House dinnerware from 1945.[33]

Mickey or Trude should have warned Mrs. Roosevelt about my huge appetite, but this would not have been polite. We were then each presented a platter of pot roast with carrots, potatoes, and peas. The peas tasted like the Le Sueur kind that came in a can. The pot roast was decent. Pot roast is tolerated by all, judged by a Jew, well-done for some; I found it not memorable, but adequate. The dinner was quickly consumed by the three diners, especially the rolls and butter, which were set on the smaller plate to the left of the main platter. I was never sure where to place the bread and butter plate. I didn't want them to think I was uncouth.

I knew this meal was trouble for Eleanor and I felt bad for the elderly maid scurrying around the table to serve us. I was certain she rarely had soon-to-be newlyweds to feed. Finally, the dessert was placed in front of me. Not a drop of whipped cream, which I had prayed for, appeared. This was a serious dinner; nothing playful about it.

---

[33] The Roosevelts used a 1,722-piece set from Lenox in the White House.

When we finished, I left my napkin by my empty plate where some pink juice from the strawberries and a few crumbs from the cake remained.

The earlier discussion with Mrs. Roosevelt left me relieved because it was over. I now felt slightly sleepy. The interview was not what I had expected. I should have been interviewing her. I had been served a conventional meal. What was I expecting for dinner? My thoughts had wandered while eating in the very dark dining room at the bridge table, covered by a little white linen cloth with lit candles, and served by Mrs. Roosevelt's housekeeper.

I put away my thoughts and decided this was a very ordinary and inadequate meal for young people.

Eleanor didn't seem to care about the food. Later, I learned she was not known to be the best cook. Although we were still hungry, I was pleased to be there because I knew I was making Trude happy. I wanted to be close to Mickey. He seemed too blond and handsome, the "Blond Prince" as my mother-in-law would call him. Mrs. Roosevelt had been a true friend to Trude to open her home and invite Mickey and me to dinner.

Did I mention we ate by candlelight? This touch amused me. This was in keeping with Eleanor's romantic effort. Was this gesture in honor of the young couple about to marry?

I knew I was making Trude happy, and Mrs. Roosevelt wanted to be close to Trude and Mickey, so her focus on me was the way to go. Also, I believe Eleanor wanted to bring herself closer to Trude and Joe. She played the older aunt role very well. So, the dinner was a success!

Here I was, eating in Mrs. Roosevelt's apartment, a far cry from Freehold, New Jersey. I accepted what was happening to me as a logical step for a young student who had graduated from Bryn Mawr College and now the only girl in my architecture class at Penn.

I was marrying not only a devoted handsome young man, but an heir to Standard Oil. Somehow nothing surprised me about myself. I seemed to naturally fit in.

I had tremendous confidence bolstered by repeated compliments for my looks, greatly embellished by my mother who had taken me shopping at every opportunity from Asbury Park to Philadelphia, and good academic standing. My mother was skilled at designing my outfits and I loved wearing them. This evening the pink Pucci dress had seemed to become my favorite, so stylish that even Jackie Kennedy would have liked it.

I was skinny then, and everything looked great on me. I recall that Diana Vreeland, editor of *Vogue* said, "You can never be too thin or too rich." I was very thin and I was about to become very rich; I just didn't know it yet.

Where was I going? I just knew I had to finish my schoolwork and become a great architect and, if possible, an archaeological architect with Mickey as my partner. He seemed to like my archaeology interests and he was proud of me. I became very comfortable with him. He seemed to love me so much and I felt more than safe with him. The apparent approval of me by Mrs. Roosevelt had me wondering what she would say to Trude about me. Whatever it was, Eleanor Roosevelt must have made a positive report.

I felt I had gently been grilled to perfection by a master. There was never a moment when I felt unworthy of my status as the soon-to-be Mrs. Roger Pratt. Mrs. Roosevelt had made me feel that no one was more appropriate than I to marry Mickey. Not once did I think there was any question of my suitability to be Mickey's wife.

It was only later that my mother told me that if I were from the Long Island Lighting family, or one comparable family, I would have been immediately accepted without an interview by one such as Mrs. Roosevelt.

Did I realize that even my mother was proud of our intellectual heritage as I was? Nothing could beat my ancestors, not even Standard Oil.

I had not considered that with money comes power and with power, social success. Money never guided my decision to marry Mickey. Perhaps it would have deterred me when I discovered how much I would need to raise two children. I always had enough. Money was not yet seen as essential in my mind.

I never knew the struggles that came with wealth and certainly did not consider that a lack of it would lead to a certain kind of difficulty. When I told Mrs. Roosevelt that my pursuit of information about the current world defined me, I must have sounded simple. As someone who loves ancient art, I identify the *Dying Gaul*[34] with the victims of the Holocaust. Now I was sitting with Mrs. Roosevelt, displaying my vast interest in archaeology. It was a surreal moment, but confusing to me as I look back on it.

I later realized what a stupid situation I was in. Mrs. Roosevelt, the queen of human rights, entertaining me for dinner while I sat silently and did not question her about why the United States did nothing to stop the Holocaust just some twenty years before? Why were Auschwitz, the chemical plants, and the rail tracks bringing the victims to be gassed never bombed by the Americans? Why was the *SS St. Louis*, carrying Jewish refugees from Europe, turned away by U.S. Coast Guard guns only to return for those passengers to be killed in the gas chambers of Auschwitz? And beyond these questions, why were the Nazis given support to come into power from the United States and American corporations?

---

[34] The *Dying Galatian* or the *Dying Gladiator* is an Ancient Roman marble copy of a lost Hellenistic sculpture thought to have been originally executed in bronze.

The Holocaust affected many, including my family. I remember going with my mother and father from Freehold to Brooklyn to visit my Aunt Lillian,[35] Uncle Morris, and their two children, Eta and Avrum, for lunch. Uncle Morris was a pharmacist and owned the Sheepshead Bay Pharmacy.

After World War II, many Jewish people were still upset and ruminating over Hitler's massacre of Jewish people. Uncle Morris came to America from Warsaw, but his parents had stayed and he lost touch with them. Somehow, he found out the tragic fate of his mother and father. I couldn't believe what I heard. He said that they had been put in the ovens in a concentration camp and killed. For the first time, I saw a fifty-year-old man cry. Tears fell down his face endlessly. It was just recently that he had been informed of his parents' deaths.

I thought nothing of all this. What should I have said? Should I have asked, "Why was nothing done by the Roosevelt administration to stop the carnage of the Holocaust?"

Should I have opened the door for her response? To my shame, I was silent.

---

[35] After World War II ended, Aunt Lillian traveled and stayed in Israel, where she settled in the West Bank. Her son would later become a rabbi.

# 40

## Leaving Eleanor's

Trying to remember the way out of Eleanor's apartment seemed easier than remembering the way in. Is this because I was relieved to be leaving? Was it because I had somehow managed to avoid the questions that really mattered? I was ashamed. I knew, however, that it was a subject that had to be avoided.

We never addressed the real issues. I recall the apartment being on the second floor with straight flights of stairs on the side. I remember thinking that Mickey must have been there before; he had no difficulty finding the exit. He was not troubled by the Holocaust issue. The more I thought about it, the worse I felt. Where was Eleanor when millions of people were being murdered?

All of this started to weigh on me when we exited Eleanor's second-floor apartment. The stairs seemed familiar to Mickey as he used them easily when we finished dinner. In fact, he seemed to dash ahead of me. He had done his duty. I thanked Eleanor profusely as Mickey told her that we were sorry we had to eat and run. We were on our way to see a movie at the Beekman Theater.

Mickey was oblivious to what was beginning to trouble me about his mother's dearest friend. I expect Eleanor reported her thoughts to Trude immediately or during their daily 7:00 a.m. phone call. I would've liked to have been a fly on the wall during that conversation. I must have done very well with my interview; there were no repercussions and the wedding proceeded in a few days.

Mrs. Roosevelt's husband, Franklin Delano Roosevelt, had been a U.S. president for nearly four terms. I was too shy to ask her what it was like to be the first lady. There was so much I could have learned from her instead of getting information from books about the Roosevelts after she was gone. Maybe Joe Lash could have prepared me somewhat for a more appropriate dinner conversation. The questions that I could have asked Eleanor as I was a guest in her home continue to haunt me.

I did not see Eleanor again until my wedding reception one week later.

Years later, a Bryn Mawr College classmate of mine, Susan Schonberg Epstein, knew a Jewish assistant to Joseph Stalin,[36] and I heard that when FDR visited the dictator, the assistant found himself alone with the American president. The assistant took the opportunity to plead for help for the Jews being annihilated. Roosevelt replied, "I did not come here to discuss that matter." How did this callous indifference slip by so many people? How was this atrocity allowed? I put this all in the back of my mind, too preoccupied with my approaching wedding.

In my closet were two white dresses, one for the wedding and one for the reception. However, beneath my happy façade, I was in

---

[36] Stalin died March 5, 1953.

pain over my repressed findings about what I viewed as Eleanor's indifference to the Holocaust. I told Mickey about my feelings about the Roosevelts and the Holocaust. He had compassion, but I know it is hard to feel the gravity of it all without having been directly impacted by the Holocaust as my family has been.

# 41

## The Wedding

I can remember being annoyed with my brother Richard's slow speed as he drove me, Mom, and Dad to the rabbi's study in Manhattan for my wedding to Mickey. Richard was so slow that I couldn't stand it! He was being cautious, making sure we got there in one piece. The wedding dress I wore was white and sleeveless with a matching jacket, one of my Nan Duskin purchases. I also wore a large, beautiful white hat decorated with artificial flowers.

Mickey had arranged for us to be married after sundown on a Saturday night in accordance with the Jewish Sabbath tradition. When we walked out of the temple, Mickey grabbed my hat and threw it in the air. After, we had a wedding dinner with just the immediate family. It was a terrific meal at one large table with about twenty people who toasted to Mickey and me. When it was time for Peter Pratt, Mickey's older brother, to toast, he said that

Mickey had picked me—a flower—from the side of the road in New Jersey.

After the wedding and the dinner, we did not see my family again until Monday for the reception at the Cosmopolitan Club in Manhattan. Mickey and I spent our wedding night at Eliot Pratt's house at 177 East 71st Street. Nobody was there except the two of us in the bedroom on the second floor.

In the morning, I woke up to the sound of trashcans rattling in front of the house. Then we went off to Connecticut to see his father, Eliot and his new wife, Trudie, on Eliot's farm in New Milford. We stayed one night. I remember coming down for breakfast the next day wearing Mickey's trousers. We were going back to New York City on Monday as I was going to Elizabeth Arden so my hair looked good for the reception. All was going well!

The guest list was amazing and included U.S. Attorney for the Southern District of New York Robert Morgenthau; Johnny Boettiger, who was Eleanor's grandson; and James and John Roosevelt, Eleanor's sons. I still have Eleanor's handwritten response to the reception invitation.

Eleanor arrived just as Mickey and I were walking into the reception. We had a brief conversation with her outside of the Cosmopolitan Club. It was still daylight at the time, and her skin appeared downy soft in the sun. I was wearing a sleeveless off-white silk shantung cocktail dress. I don't remember what she was wearing. But I do recall her long black limousine parked in front of the club. She did not stay long.

Thinking back, having dinner with Eleanor was like having dinner with Cleopatra. I didn't know either very well. I only knew of Eleanor as the wife of Franklin Delano Roosevelt.

Now reading about most of Eleanor's friends, it seems a large age gap existed between her and her other confidants, like David

Gurewitsch. Trude's twenty-four year age difference was something of a norm for the former first lady, not a unique feature of their friendship. I felt like such a kid.

# 42

## Honeymoon

I received so many gifts, especially after the Cosmopolitan Club reception. All I kept thinking was that I had so many thank-you notes to write! What do other brides do? What I recall most is that our wedding gift from Eleanor was a pair of silver candelabras, which I received when we returned from our honeymoon. She should not have been concerned with whether I'd like them or not. I loved them right away, of course, and used them on my dinner table. I've used them every chance I've had and for meals as well, especially pot roast.

All of my thank-you notes, including the one to Eleanor, were somewhat late due to a long honeymoon, which got longer and longer not because of a dreaded return to architecture school, but because we were having so much fun in Paris, Italy, and Greece. Years later, when I visited Hyde Park, I had a quick pang that I would see my thank-you note displayed with Eleanor's memorabilia. Instead, I found many gifts that Eleanor received from Joe

*Candelabra wedding gift to Helen and Roger (1962).*

Lash. This surprised me and only when I found out about the relationship between Joe and Eleanor did it seem appropriate.

Mickey and I were very anxious to take off on our wedding trip.

The *SS Rotterdam* left the port with my family waving goodbye from the dock. The two of us were alone with each other. We were amazed at the wonderful accommodations that had been arranged by the U.S. Trust Company.

Finally, I could think of our trip and how wonderful it would be. Just the journey to Europe was going to be luxurious, spending five days on the Atlantic Ocean eating sumptuous meals in first-class dining. Roger, whom I called Mickey, had made all the plans and I knew he was going to take me to the places I had learned about in my archaeology classes with Professor Mellink at Bryn Mawr. In addition, I was going to visit his family in Konstanz, West Germany.

*Honeymoon on the
SS Rotterdam on
the Atlantic Ocean
(1962).*

We were supposed to land in Le Havre, France, but there was a strike, so the ship took us to Rotterdam instead. From there, we traveled by train to Paris. When we arrived in Paris, we went straight to the Lotte Hotel, which was popular with the Pratt family. I remember their sheets were made of linen and made my skin itch. I wonder if they still use those same damned sheets.

Mickey loved high-quality food, so we ate a lot during our honeymoon. The one gift of being a newlywed at the age of twenty-three was that I didn't gain an ounce of weight throughout the entire trip.

I distinctly remember sitting in the Louvre Museum and seeing the Victory Statue at the top of the steps. I also remember the large pool in the Tuileries Garden where you could rent little sailboats.

Years later, I took my daughters to the same place and rented sailboats with them.

Mickey and I rented a Volkswagen Beetle with a manual transmission and we made our way to Konstanz. We stopped at the border and I suddenly felt very Jewish and afraid of the German guards at the crossing. They wanted to see our papers and to check our passports. And they asked us a lot of questions about where we were going.

When they finally let us through, we proceeded on our way to Mickey's grandmother's house. It seemed like the whole family lived in that house. We stayed there for a few days, and during that time we went to a public swimming beach on Lake Constance and enjoyed local cuisine in German restaurants. Mickey's younger cousin ordered raw hamburger with raw egg on top of it. I can't say that it appealed to my American taste buds. Instead, I enjoyed Wiener schnitzel. But the little boy eating raw meat and eggs captivated me.

One day we visited Zurich, which was close to Konstanz, and had a *Kaffee mit Schlag*, which is coffee with whipped cream. I had this drink many times throughout our honeymoon. I loved it.

Following our visit to Konstanz, we had to cross the Alps into Italy. I never thought or expected the Alps to be warm and pleasant, but they had gorgeous weather when we passed through in June. We stopped at Lake Como, where we stayed at a quaint pink stucco hotel with very high ceilings. Parked in front of the hotel was the most fantastic red Ferrari.

Before leaving for our honeymoon, I hadn't been feeling very well. After our wedding reception, I had seen my Uncle Frank, who was a doctor. He referred me to a gynecologist. During my visit, the gynecologist, a practicing Catholic, had suggested that we use the rhythm method as birth control. When I got a second opinion, another gynecologist suggested I have a minor surgery to remove a Bartholin's cyst. I would have to change the wound dressing regularly while on my honeymoon. It seemed as if both doctors were conspiring to make sure that I did not have sex on my honeymoon.

In spite of my health issues, Mickey and I managed to see as many cathedrals and restaurants that two young people could. I especially remember visiting Notre Dame in Paris. I adored the rose window, which reminded me of my grandmother's stained glass work that she had told me about at a synagogue in Bremen, Germany.

Eventually, all of my health problems were resolved and we began to fully enjoy our honeymoon. Driving into Rome at night, we were dazzled by the city lights. We stayed in Rome for ten days. We saw a Bernini colonnade, the Sistine Chapel, and sat on the Spanish Steps, where I didn't see a single familiar face. The food was fantastic and I had my first dandelion weed salad. Fortunately, there was an Elizabeth Arden salon in Rome. There, I had my hair done and my very first professional pedicure. While in Rome, I also had my first pair of custom shoes made.

After Rome, we flew to Athens. This was my very first time on a plane. My jangled nerves were tempered by Mickey, who stayed by my side. His knowledge of Europe came from his many previous trips there. The Athenian airport looked disheveled, nothing like Rome's international airport.

My recent degree in archaeology and courses in architecture prepared me for a fascinating and exciting trip to Athens. It would be a visual feast. In Athens, we stayed in an apartment near the American School for Classical Studies. One morning, I went out and bought olive oil, eggplant, and onions to prepare as I had seen the local women doing. I cut up the eggplants, scooped out the insides, filled them with onions, and baked them. I had stopped by

*Mickey and Helen on honeymoon, Parthenon, Athens, Greece (1962).*

the local bakery for a fresh loaf of bread. Sadly, Mickey did not like the eggplant.

We headed to the Athens Acropolis and looked for all the important details that I had learned from Professor Mellink. Going through the Propylaea, the gateway to the Acropolis, I was breathless. My eyes were filled with everything I read and saw in William Bell Dinsmore's *Greek Architecture*. It was all coming to life. It was amazing that I was actually there. This was truly the best wedding gift that Mickey could give me. It was here that I noticed the "father and grandfather" of the Parthenon: traces of the levels that lay beneath it.

Mickey rented another Volkswagen and we went to see Mycenae and Tiryns, which were not well known at the time and were hardly ever visited. The Acropolis Museum was a chock-full of pottery and sculpture. My one regret is that we didn't go to Delphi, which I later wrote about in one of my books. But we did visit Agamemnon's Tomb at Mycenae.

Mickey and I had so much in common that we never ran out of conversation. I started to like being a married woman and I knew I had done the right thing by marrying him.

While in Greece, we also visited Crete, home to some of the world's most important archaeological ruins. I had the chance to see Knossos, Phaistos, and Mallia. We took an overnight ship from Piraeus to Heraklion, the capital of Crete, through the choppy waters of the Aegean Sea. A few years later, I heard the same ship had sunk. When we landed in Heraklion, we went to our hotel, which was managed by a very stern woman who never smiled. After the boat trip, we just barely managed to hold down our dinner. When we went to the city center that evening, incredibly I saw someone I never expected to see. It was my beloved former Professor Mellink. There she was, standing tall in a crowd. I ran right over to her and the three of us ended up spending the night together eating and drinking. She had been on her way to Azerbaijan and decided to stop in Greece. Not only was Professor Mellink my archaeological professor at Bryn Mawr, but she was the one who encouraged me to pursue an architecture career. Without her, I never would have met Mickey. I never would have had the chance to sit across from Eleanor Roosevelt at a dinner table.

Throughout my honeymoon, there was one memory that kept replaying in my mind. It was what Eleanor had said to me when I greeted her at my reception: "Go take care of your other guests." I couldn't help but feel that I should take care of her. Eleanor's gentleness and kindness amazed me and my friends. Susie Epstein kept Eleanor occupied, so I didn't feel guilty about leaving her alone. Susie had jumped at the chance to speak to the former first lady. Eleanor was beginning to feel to me like a grandmother who need to be carefully attended. I kept reviewing all this and hoped that I would soon be a woman as independent as Eleanor. I thought that my architecture degree would one day provide me with the security that Eleanor had. I expected that it would give me the opportunities that Eleanor and Trude enjoyed.

# 43

## Returning to Philadelphia

After the honeymoon, we returned to Philadelphia, where we would look for an apartment. We found one that we painted white. We added interior stair railings and from the kitchen window, I could see the Rittenhouse Swim Club just across the street. The swim club had been designed by my architecture professor, Tim Vreeland, and had received national awards. I would hang a dish towel from the back window of our apartment to signal to Mickey that dinner was ready.

The candelabras were a focal point in our new home. They must have first arrived at Trude and Joe's house. I only remember a Tiffany box, which I opened during one of my many visits to Trude and Joe's home in the Village after our honeymoon. Trude had told me how much Eleanor fussed over the purchase and hoped I would like them. Of course I liked them. I clearly remember Mrs. Roosevelt's concern. If she knew the whole story today about the candelabras, she would have been even more concerned about where they would be headquartered.

I even suspect the candelabras had not been purchased for us but might have been from Eleanor's family silver collection, the Livingston collection in Hyde Park, New York. Livingston was Eleanor's great-great-grandfather.

The gift of the candelabras may have been the result of Eleanor's need to be close to Trude and Joe, and I got swept along with the many efforts she had made to shower us with gifts. Even before our marriage, during the dinner at her home, she gave a more personal gift of a pair of beige silk pajamas to Mickey. I guess the candelabras were a gift we could both enjoy. Did she think the same thing? The gift given to me at the same time Mickey received the pajamas was a keychain she had brought back from Israel.

When we moved from our apartment at 1938 Lombard Street to a house we purchased at 1914 Panama Street in Philadelphia in 1965, I brought the Eleanor memorabilia—the candelabras and the keychain—with me.

Now, fifty years later, the candelabras are still my responsibility. However, recently they had to recover from an expensive repair after breaking during an excessive polishing.

In 2014, the candelabras were being cleaned by Shefteq, a steward at the Franklin Inn Club in Philadelphia, and each arm broke off at the stem when he enthusiastically polished them. No regrets from Shefteq. If only he had known who had given them to me, how important to me and how important they were to Eleanor.

If only he knew how badly Mrs. Roosevelt would have felt. They were so important that they were featured in my divorce papers from Mickey. The question: who would get the candelabras? Dare I say, they got a whole sentence in our divorce agreement. Did the children get as much? Mickey wanted the candelabras for himself, but he stopped insisting when I said I would give them to our daughters, Suzanne and Elizabeth, when I die. One would go to each girl. In the meantime, I am stuck with their polishing.

Now, as I write this, the candelabras are mended. Mickey is dead, leaving behind another wife and family. The candelabras are all mine and will ultimately go to the girls. Mrs. Roosevelt's candelabras are presently safe in my dining room. They have never looked so good—mended, polished, and worthy of being photographed. Unfortunately, Mrs. Roosevelt, Trude, my mother, and my father are also gone. I am the only one remaining in the family, other than the girls, to admire them.

I briefly think I should have a dinner to honor them and their survival. Maybe at the Franklin Inn Club. Perhaps we would have the same meal that was served by Eleanor for dinner. Would anyone like pot roast?

This story of Mrs. Roosevelt shows that nothing is simple; the price of ownership is often very high, and I'm still at my desk looking over at the candelabras that came from Mrs. Roosevelt.

Trude wanted approval from Eleanor for Mickey's marriage to me. What else was the whole dinner about? I took Mrs. Roosevelt's dinner as part of the wedding celebration, which it was. In my mind, there was no doubt that the wedding would occur. I, being the bride, could not believe anyone disapproved of the marriage, especially Eleanor. Though, I did suspect that my family was accommodating me with their approval.

Did I expect that my dear Uncle Frank Niemtzow would not like it? Why would I? He said to me, "Now you can take care of your parents" when I called him to announce my engagement to Mickey. What did he mean?

The wealth of the Pratts did not flow as if from a spigot, especially, as I would find out if I wanted a divorce, from the ardent lover, Mickey, who would become the reluctant man who cast aside his responsibilities for his wife and children.

When I was sitting in Eleanor's New York living room in 1962, alone with her and Mickey, I could have asked so much of Mrs. Roosevelt. Were you nervous before you married FDR? Will it be too difficult for me to join the Pratt family as a Jew?

Later, I received a beautiful wall hanging that once belonged to Eleanor. It was gifted to me by Trude Lash in 1970. Since then, the tapestry has hung in my Panama Street home. First, in the bedroom Mickey and I shared, and presently it is in the second-floor den. Somehow, I have never been able to find the right place for it.

The research I've done on the tapestry suggests it was a gift to Eleanor from Norway's Trygve Lie, the first secretary-general of the United Nations. Why do I think that Trude wanted to get rid of it? She had invited Mickey and me to a dinner at her house, where she gave me the tapestry. Mickey and I split in 1971, just a year after receiving it. Trude went upstairs after dinner and emerged with it in her arms, a bulky, folded-up rectangle of fabric. She looked at me and said, "I want you to have this."

Holding on to the bundle, I took it, not really having another option and not entirely sure what it was, or what I was going to do with it. But if your mother-in-law hands you a gift, you don't say no, especially when she was so insistent. It seems she wanted it out of the house, and I will never know why. The entire way home to Philadelphia, with the bundle clutched in my arms, I just kept thinking, "Where am I going to put this?"

Later, I learned that Eleanor collected tapestries. I do not remember seeing her collection at Hyde Park, though I visited there with my children, Suzanne and Elizabeth.

Presently, I have placed my small collection of Eleanor gifts, except the tapestry and Mickey's pajamas, in a special place called a tokonoma by the Japanese. It is a recessed space for valuables and treasured items, such as my gifts from Eleanor. When I visited Japan in 1964 for the Olympics, I learned that even TV sets were placed in a home's tokonoma.

# 44

## The Eleuthera Vacation

In December 1962, Mickey and I asked Trude and Joe to recommend an interesting place for a Christmas vacation. They suggested the Potlatch Club on the island of Eleuthera in the Bahamas.

When we boarded the plane, there were Trude and Joe, already seated. We were shocked. It was not a kind thing to do to newlyweds. We needed some private time to recover from the stress of graduate school. I always had the slightest suspicion that Trude was trying to break us up.

Every day in Eleuthera, she would send Mickey out on a fishing trip, which left me alone with her. While he fished, I painted watercolors, and I signed every one with a black heart. I was spending more time with my mother-in-law than my new husband.

A memorable lunch during our vacation was with Trude and Peggy Guggenheim.[37] They were loud and had been drinking and were tossing several nasty, barb-like toasts at one another. Trude kept ordering me to get various dishes for her from the buffet. Finally, I got so offended that I told her to get them herself.

One night, I had to return a book to Trude in her island cottage, which was just one room. She and Joe were in twin beds. Trude's bed was closest to the door. She let me in, got back in bed, and said, "Joe is letting me sleep with him." What a strange remark. Why was Trude compelled to say this? Was she trying to confide in me or let me in on the status of their marriage? I will never know. In hindsight, maybe the comment sheds light on the arrangement of Joe and Trude's marriage by Eleanor.

---

[37] The Guggenheims had a vast art collection and endowed the Guggenheim Museum in New York and another in Venice.

# 45

## The Legacy

After WWII and its treachery and abuse of humanity, there was a dire need for a declaration of human rights to protect humanity from a repeat of the horrors that the world was subjected to in the Holocaust.

In 1948, the United Nations adopted "The Universal Declaration of Human Rights." Eleanor Roosevelt chaired the committee that drafted the articles of the Declaration, which was the highlight for the UN post-1945.

Unfortunately, the world has not been ready or willing to accommodate this document entirely. Even in 2018, as I write about Eleanor, I have been aghast at the violence of the Syrian regime under Bashar al-Assad and their use of chemical weapons. Every act of violence is disgusting depending on one's perspective. "If man is destructive by nature," Ian McHarg, a professor of landscape architecture at the University of Pennsylvania once said, "One has to remain constantly vigilant to protect against such violence."

Eleanor was so aware of this dilemma and struggled in the hope that "The Universal Declaration of Human Rights" would accomplish something tangible. But the battle is constant.

While I was in architecture school, two very important people in our history passed away: Eleanor Roosevelt and John F. Kennedy. When Eleanor died in November of 1962, I crowded around the radio with several of my classmates in the architecture studio at the University of Pennsylvania, awaiting the dreaded news. We knew that she was very sick and that her passing was imminent. We were very upset. Only years later did I realize that the dinner at Mrs. Roosevelt's apartment was a most extraordinary event. Eleanor was America's queen. I never think about my alma mater without thinking of that occasion in 1962, listening to the announcer proclaim Eleanor's passing. I don't recall if Mickey was there in school with me at that time. It felt like we had just lost an older aunt. I felt close to her through her special dinner for Mickey and me and the spectacular wedding gift she gave us.

When JFK was assassinated, I was on my way to architecture school when I heard mumblings about his shooting. My baby nurse, who was watching Suzanne, had arrived at my apartment very upset. She said something had happened to the president, but wasn't sure what. I quickly turned on the television and heard that JFK had been shot. They were chasing three people up the grassy knoll in Dallas along the parade route. To this day, it is still unclear who actually shot the president.

# *Epilogue*

On April 12, 1945, Franklin Delano Roosevelt died after serving four terms in office. It was not until his death that Eleanor learned of the existence of the Manhattan Project.[38] On August 5, 1945, the first atomic bomb dropped on Hiroshima. On October 24, 1945, six months after FDR's death, two months after the atomic bombs, the United Nations came into existence.

President Roosevelt's successor, Harry S. Truman, appointed Eleanor as chair of the United Nations' Humans Rights Commission in late 1945. The commission set out to draft "The Universal Declaration of Human Rights." It was drafted December 10, 1948. One of the main provisions of the Declaration was the universal abolishment of poverty.[39]

I was just a young girl in Freehold, New Jersey when Eleanor was put in charge of the UN's Human Rights Committee. My grandmother Channah was still alive and living in Philadelphia. But, she would not live to know the woman I would become—the

---

[38] The Manhattan Project was a secret military project that created the first nuclear weapon for the U.S. in 1942. It was based in Manhattan, New York.

[39] In 2018, Philadelphia and Camden, New Jersey, across the river, led the U.S. in child poverty; one of four children are impoverished.

first female to attend Penn's architecture school and a member of a prominent American family. In writing this book, I often wondered what Channah would have thought of my dinner with Eleanor. Perhaps she would have said, "Only in America can your granddaughter eat pot roast with a former First Lady."

Surely, I inherited at least some of Channah's strength and character, and hopefully Eleanor recognized those traits in me. Knowing what Eleanor went through, bearing so much power and responsibility, I was struck by her constant kindness and sense of duty to help others. I made a special effort to speak to Mrs. Roosevelt at my wedding reception and when I finally did, she told me to "Go take care of the other guests, don't worry about me."

I had been unnecessarily concerned when I met Eleanor in 1962. Eleanor was selfless and always focused her concern on the rest of the world. She acted to protect others instead of herself. Eleanor gave her approval of my marriage to Roger Sherman Pratt and acknowledged it when talking to Trude Lash and relaying that we seemed simpatico with each other. Eleanor gave several gifts to us, particularly the two sterling silver candelabras for the wedding, a keychain from Israel, and a pair of beige silk pajamas for Mickey. Eleanor seemed very invested in our wedding. Was she identifying with us, a young couple, as we related to the beginning years of her marriage to Franklin?

Eleanor had not received the same approval or fanfare for her marriage to FDR as I did for my wedding, and was reportedly treated rather poorly by her mother-in-law, Sara Roosevelt. Maybe my marriage to Mickey was her opportunity to show how things should be handled. Eleanor showed generosity, acceptance, and was welcoming to someone who was Jewish, which was very different from her Episcopalian roots. That being said, the Jewish faith was not foreign to her, as Eleanor was a close friend of Joe

Lash. In the wake of the Holocaust, being a Jew was not easy. I felt as if I always had to prove myself to be worthy of what I said. What came with being Jewish was the necessity to try harder than others to succeed.

However, the big question remains. Would Eleanor have sat quietly by or interrupted the divorce between Mickey and me, ten years after she initially gave her approval for our marriage? I would hope that she would have said something to Mickey, that she would have stuck up for me. It was a big deal for Mickey and me to have a private dinner and the personal stamp of approval from Eleanor. I took that honor with me into our marriage. Also, was Trude betraying her relationship with Eleanor by marrying Joe? Did the Russians succeed in using Trude as an asset?

In Adlai Stevenson's address to the UN in memory of Eleanor, he described her legacy by saying, "The power of her words come from the depth of her conviction." I agreed, and I thought that Eleanor was a true altruist. The world is a better place to have had Anna Eleanor Roosevelt in it. I am fortunate to have been her guest for dinner that night.